Praise for Visions, Values, and Corporate Hypocrisy

"One of the best books gaining interest during the great resignation movement..."

—Lisa Quinn, *Newsfile Corp.*

"Extremely valuable, digestible insight. All graduates need to read to prepare themselves for what could be waiting for them on the other side of their diploma. Also, a must read for all leadership to help them avoid the hypocrisy of corporate America."

—David S., Amazon Verified Buyer

"*Visions, Values, and Corporate Hypocrisy* could not be written at a better time. Authentic leadership is under attack from every angle..."

—Madeline Carr, Librarian

"...an enjoyable read...well written. Thanks Dr. Williams for exposing the dark side of organizational life, and promoting the many advantages of authentic leadership."

—G. Dumigan, Management Consultant

"A very engaging book that should be shared with seasoned leaders and employees in order to promote awareness and shine a bright light on how strategy and culture can be sacrificed without regard to long-term consequences on businesses, employees and consumers."

—Vincent J., PhD, Amazon Verified Buyer

"...a well written work that addresses the destructive nature of do-as-I-say, not-as-I-do leadership in organizations today."

—Ed Patterson, Ed D., Amazon Verified Buyer

Visions, Values, and Corporate Hypocrisy

VISIONS, VALUES, AND CORPORATE HYPOCRISY

the hijacking of corporate conscience

KENDALL E. WILLIAMS, PhD

gatekeeper press

Columbus, Ohio

The views and opinions expressed in this book are solely those of the author and do not reflect the views or opinions of Gatekeeper Press. Gatekeeper Press is not to be held responsible for and expressly disclaims responsibility of the content herein.

Visions, Values, and Corporate Hypocrisy: the hijacking of corporate conscience

Published by Gatekeeper Press
2167 Stringtown Rd, Suite 109
Columbus, OH 43123-2989
www.GatekeeperPress.com

Copyright © 2021 by Kendall Williams
All rights reserved. Neither this book, nor any parts within it may be sold or reproduced in any form or by any electronic or mechanical means, including information storage and retrieval systems, without permission in writing from the author. The only exception is by a reviewer, who may quote short excerpts in a review.

The cover design, interior formatting, typesetting, and editorial work for this book are entirely the product of the author. Gatekeeper Press did not participate in and is not responsible for any aspect of these elements.

ISBN (paperback): 9781662916892
eISBN: 9781662916908

DEDICATION

This book is dedicated to my three young adults; Ryan Mychal, Reid Matthew, and Kayla Marie Williams. Each of you have inspired me in a special way.

Ryan, my first born, your tenacious pursuit of your own personal goals, and your meticulous planning provided that extra motivation for me to stay the course with this book. Your musical talent is simply incomparable!

Reid, my tiger, I will always be in awe of your superior mental and physical aptitude, and I admire your compassionate heart more than I can say. You are blessed with more than your fair share of talent...the world is your oyster!

Kayla, my beautiful princess, I'm so proud of your kind nature, and academic accomplishments. You have laid the foundation for great successes in life. Your tenderness and zest for learning have always been an inspiration.

The three of you mean everything to me, and there are no words that can adequately express my love for you.

CONTENTS

1. HYPOCRITE LEADERS — 1
2. AUTHENTIC LEADERSHIP — 11
3. THE VALUE OF VALUES — 23
4. POLITICAL CORRECTNESS AT WORK — 31
5. HYPOCRISY IN THE WOKE CULTURE — 39
6. DIVERSITY AND INCLUSION: THE MYTH — 45
7. TOKENISM AND THE INCLUSION ILLUSION — 51
8. HYPOCRISY IN HUMAN RESOURCES — 61
9. THE UNPLEASANT CONSEQUENCES OF HYPOCRISY — 73
10. THE DARK SIDE OF "EI" — 81
11. TRUTH-TELLING AIN'T EASY — 87
12. WHY ACTIONS MATTER MORE THAN WORDS — 95

ABOUT THE AUTHOR — 103
REFERENCES — 105

ACKNOWLEDGMENTS

Exposing one's private thoughts to public debate can be onerous, especially when those thoughts challenge conventional leadership methodology. Yet had it not been for the example of two outstanding leaders that I encountered earlier in my career, the context of this book might never have occurred to me.

The first of these is Deb Raco-Bechtold, she was Vice President for a large U.S. cable television provider. Not only does Deb have a true passion for people and a "people first" mentality, she is also an authentic leader who never compromises her value system. Her unwavering confidence, optimism, and resilience have been a continual source of inspiration, for which I owe her my warmest thanks. Finally, many thanks to June Simmons, a nationally recognized leader in the healthcare space, and CEO/co-founder of Partners in Care Foundation. I had the pleasure of building June's contact center operation designed to further her company mission.

As a tireless, and purpose-driven leader, June is uncompromising in her commitment to lead authentically, and she insists the same of her organizational members. June's leadership style embodies all the key tenets of this book...she sets the standards by which other leaders should be measured.

I consider myself immensely privileged to have worked with these outstanding leaders, and owe my passion for developing authentic corporate cultures to their example.

INTRODUCTION

The setting was a stuffy, windowless conference room at a Marriott hotel in Greenville, South Carolina. Tired and weary, I was nearing the end of a marathon of intense interviews as I was meeting with the organization's search committee. I was the prime candidate for a top role at a nearby 1,000-seat contact center, and the committee wanted to ensure no stones were left unturned. This all-day session was the culmination of an eight-month search for a proven candidate with the "right" knowledge and skills to turn around a dysfunctional organization.

The Greenville location hosted 700 front-line employees, over 200 managers and supervisors, and garnered $50 million in annual revenues from major, Fortune 500 client companies. At the time I was solicited to interview, the organization was deeply mired in a wide range of issues, including widespread employee theft (which led to the loss of millions of dollars in revenues), a slew of disgruntled Fortune 500 clients, disengaged workers, declining morale, rising absenteeism, unprecedented employee attrition, *dishonest leadership,* and a host of other challenging issues that would discourage even the most courageous leader.

I knew this career move would bring tremendous pressure into my life, and the lives of my two teenage sons who were forced to uproot from their familiar and comfortable surroundings in Chicago, Illinois, to the dark and desolate highways of Greenville, South Carolina, where vestiges of its racist past are memorialized with confederate flags and an abundance of graveyards hosting the remains of former slaves. But the problems I would face would be enough to keep me focused for the duration of my stay. I accepted the position with an altruistic mindset, determined to transform this once-thriving contact center. As the largest employer in the poverty-stricken city of Greenville, massive layoffs would prove disastrous to the local economy.

As I began the arduous task of unraveling the mess that I knowingly inherited, I was amazed at the glaring misalignment between the actions and behaviors of the leaders and the values that were touted in the company's employee handbook: "Our associate's personal commitment to the highest business and ethical standards and performance are what has earned us the well-deserved reputation as a leading global provider..." The company's core values were: "Be Ethical, Build Trust, Work Together, and Wow Customers." The problem is, the actions and behaviors of the leaders and employees were wildly inconsistent with the flowery words etched in the core values.

Fraudulent sales, misappropriation of client revenues, theft, and sexual harassment were the motus operandi, all masterminded by the top leaders. These nefarious and unscrupulous activities led to a wave of unpleasant outcomes, including negative press, low employee engagement, high attrition, and the loss of three major client accounts. The wide range of circumstances that nearly led to the demise of this Greenville location were directly attributable to hypocritical leadership. The results of corporate hypocrisy can be costly, and so are the managerial countermeasures which must be established to combat them, including elaborate control measures, punitive action, closer supervision, replacing terminated employees, and so on.

Since I began my career in leadership and consulting, I have had the opportunity to speak with many leaders in organizations of all sizes, and the question I am repeatedly asked is, "what is the single-most important key for successful leadership?" My answer: Be authentic! Ethics and morals can't be delegated by leaders. And when they attempt to do so, they send a message to employees of "ethics for thee, but not for me." The ability to lead authentically inspires employees to contribute their personal best toward the goals of the organization. Throughout this book, I will share insights gained throughout more than twenty years of fixing messes created by hypocritical leaders who failed to connect with the very people they are responsible for leading.

Chapter 1 opens with defining hypocrisy, and examines how this nefarious quality has wormed its way into corporate culture. Authentic leaders may be a rare breed, but genuine, transparent leadership reaps long-term benefits, as discussed in chapter 2.

Chapter 3 delves into the disparities between company values and corporate culture, while chapters 4 through 7 focus on equality, diversity, and ethical initiatives. Language and deception inform the themes of chapters 8 through 11, where the negative effects of HR jargon, inconsistent values, emotional intelligence (EI), and the psychology of lying are respectively discussed.

A core message throughout this book is that integrity is not born out of what we say, but out of what we do. This argument is brought to a head in the final chapter, which emphasizes the importance of acting in accordance with the values we set out. In other words, leaders must "walk the walk" and not simply "talk the talk" when it comes to driving company initiatives and setting an example for others to follow.

1

HYPOCRITE LEADERS

"When you do a charitable deed, do not sound a trumpet before you as the hypocrites do in the streets, that they may have glory from men"

- Matthew 6:2 KJV

*E*VIDENCE OF HYPOCRISY IS EVERYWHERE IN THE BUSINESS DISCOURSE. In these times of political turmoil, alternative facts, and mounting racial tension, one thing is hard to deny; there's a lot of deception in the air, and it's even more pronounced in the workplace. Some leaders seem to feel that leadership is mostly about image and appearances. When they achieve the coveted role of leader, they do their level best to look and act the part. They work hard to lure their followers with fake sincerity, but they're no more authentic than a Rolex watch purchased from a sidewalk vendor in New York City.

WHAT IS HYPOCRISY?

We all know people, and leaders, who exhibit hypocritical behavior. They make rules to apply only to others, they live one way in public, yet another in private. They knowingly manipulate the truth, they conceal details to avoid embarrassment, and they find creative and convincing ways to compensate for a weak line of reasoning. Hypocrites often know the real truth, but they're afraid that revealing it could have negative consequences, so they resort to deceptive discourse. They're so dishonest, they can be called pathological liars.

Michael Gerson (2016), an op-ed columnist for the Washington Post defines hypocrisy as "the conscious use of a mask to fool others in order to gain some benefit." In other words, hypocrites pretend to be something they are not. The word is rooted in the Greek term *hypókrisis,* meaning "to play a part, or pretend." Hypocrisy comes in at least two forms: 1. Deceiving and misleading others; and 2. Deceiving or being untrue to oneself. The first type is abominable. It's an intentional act to fool others into believing you're something that you're not. The second type can be dismissed as an acute, and perhaps unintentional lack of self-awareness. Since leaders play such a crucial role in establishing the social structures of their organizations, the form of hypocrisy is largely irrelevant, because the impact is the same.

SIGNS OF A HYPOCRITE LEADER

Anyone who has been in the corporate world for any number of years has likely encountered pathological hypocrites who bark orders down from their cozy perch. Hypocrite leaders can be quite skillful at grooming their followers to becoming hyper-aware of their own shortcomings, while turning a blind eye toward their own. Some can be narcissistic, self-promoters who engage in a predictable pattern of self-adulation, blame, and ridicule. Frank Sonnenberg (2019), an award-winning author and well-known advocate for moral character, personal values, and personal responsibility identified 23 ways to spot hypocrites:

1. They say one thing but do another.
2. They treat those in power differently than they act toward underlings.
3. They give advice but fail to follow their own guidance.
4. They preach tolerance but judge others who don't conform to their way of thinking.
5. They volunteer others but rarely raise their own hand.
6. They live one way in public but another in private.
7. They pretend to be someone they're not merely to gain acceptance from others.
8. They make rules but fail to follow the rules themselves.
9. They preach morality but live a shameful life.

10. They demand things of others that they're unwilling to do themselves.

11. They say one thing to someone's face but another thing behind their back.

12. They pretend to be wealthy even though their bank account is bare.

13. They alter their opinion to gain acceptance from people with differing viewpoints.

14. They condemn the actions of others even though they commit those same acts themselves.

15. They promote a holier-than-thou image merely to offset reckless behavior.

16. They help people only when it's in their personal interest to do so.

17. They pretend to care when their motive is really self-serving.

18. They demand austerity from others but handsomely compensate themselves.

19. They feign outrage even though they have no intention of doing anything about it.

20. They penalize some folks for wrongdoings but look the other way for others.

21. They lecture people about morality but cover up for their friends.

22. They judge others but call people intolerant when they're personally judged.

23. They act one way when folks are looking; the opposite when they're not.

Hypocrisy has been around since the beginning of time. The Bible is filled with references to hypocrisy. Jesus urged us not to be so prideful and convinced of our own goodness that we criticize others from a position of self-righteousness. In the Sermon on the Mount, Jesus said,

Why do you look at the speck of sawdust in your brother's eye and pay no attention to the plank in your own eye? You hypocrite, first take the plank out of your own eye, and then you will see clearly to remove the speck from your brother's eye (Matthew 7:3-5 NIV)

When we think of hypocrisy, a number of examples pop into our minds. Maybe it's a politician implicated in a scandal, a religious leader dishonoring the church, or a business leader swindling millions of dollars from unsuspecting victims. In the modern age of social media and 24-hour news cycles, examples of hypocrisy are far more common, and they exist in our churches, schools, civic organizations, and our local, state, and federal governments. Hypocrisy has reached pandemic proportions, and there's no sign of things slowing down.

In September of 2018, the Los Angeles City Attorney fined Wells Fargo $185 million, alleging that more than two million bank accounts were opened without the customers' consent or knowledge (Hamilton, 2016). The company was further accused of preying on vulnerable groups, such as the elderly and young college students. The irony is that page one of the company's 2015 Annual Report bears the mission, "to satisfy our customers' financial needs and help them succeed financially." As we will see in later chapters, Wells Fargo is not alone in allegedly engaging in behaviors that directly contradict the company values.

At the onset of the COVID-19 pandemic in 2020, President Trump dismissed criticism of his handling of the crisis as a democratic "hoax", and a political conspiracy concocted by Democrats. He attacked the "fake news" media, accusing them of politicizing the global pandemic, and putting out "disinformation" (Bardella, 2020). Ironically, Trump's dismissal of COVID-19 as a hoax came to an abrupt halt when he was hospitalized in October 2020 for "severe symptoms" of the virus. Throughout the Summer and Fall of 2014, Trump sent over 100 tweets criticizing the Obama Administration's handling of the Ebola crisis (see the Trump Twitter Archive). The tweets included a barrage of disparaging comments about Obama, calling him "incompetent" and "stupid." Trump even suggested that Obama "personally embrace all people in the US who contract Ebola!" (quoted in Bardella, 2020).

In the age of social media, it's easy to find stories of hypocritical politicians who have broken the public trust. Before he became president, Donald Trump railed against Barack Obama for his excessive use of executive powers. Today, Trump is criticized for doing the same. Democrats aren't immune to hypocrisy either. President Obama levied massive drone attacks against militants and terrorists, but when Trump ordered the killing by drone of Iraqi Major General Qassem Solemani, who was responsible for taking the lives of countless Americans, Democrats cried foul. Yet these same Democrats were conspicuously silent when Obama used the same tactics.

HYPOCRISY AND MOTIVE

Some hypocritical behavior is intentional, and some is unintentional. But the motive behind hypocrisy matters only to a small extent. Leaders who unintentionally engage in hypocritical behavior may simply be "bad" leaders. They likely have bad managerial skills, and they've deceived themselves into believing their leadership skills are sufficient at best, and superior, at worst. The flaws in "bad" leaders are often due to their incompetence. In addition to lacking the requisite skills to effectively lead others, they are usually unable or unwilling to reflect on their actions, assess their behaviors, and commit to self-improvement. However, even though their leadership style can be destructive to employees, they don't necessarily torment them deliberately.

On the opposite side, there are leaders who purposely deceive others for some sort of personal gain. This brand of hypocrisy is toxic and deplorable. Manipulation and deception are the modus operandi. While there are some distinct and unique traits of toxic leaders, many have perfected the art of hiding their ill intentions to ensure that their followers continue to tolerate and remain loyal to them. In reality, the most devout followers of toxic leaders are often blind to the brazen acts of their leader, and they conveniently ignore, and perhaps excuse, their obvious incompetence and greed.

One of the myths of toxic leadership is that it's short-lived because people won't tolerate hostile work environments. This is untrue for two key reasons; First, many toxic leaders are high producers. Since we live in an achievement-oriented society, they escape punishment by delivering results. We value *how much* is accomplished, rather than *how* it was accomplished. The second reason why toxic leaders often escape retribution is the fear factor. Toxic leaders are notorious for settling scores, which discourages employees from blowing the whistle. In many cases, there is no one to blow the whistle to.

THE EYE OF THE BEHOLDER

The reality is, people aren't 100% rational or consistent when it comes to making value judgments about their leaders. Hypocrisy is in the eye of the beholder. People tend to turn a blind eye to hypocrisy when it's consistent with their personal worldview. For instance, "We Build the Wall" was a non-profit organization seeking donations to build private sections of a wall along the Mexico-U.S. border to deter Mexicans from illegally entering the United States, a solemn campaign pledge by Donald Trump during his 2016 presidential run. Some argue that the notion of building a wall to shut off would-be migrants is in direct conflict with the words inscribed on Lady Liberty "bring me your tired, your poor, your huddled masses yearning to breathe free..." This group perceives the notion of a wall as a harsh and inhumane judgment of others fleeing oppression in search of a better life. But for staunch supporters of President Trump, stemming the "huddled masses" from entering the United States, whether legally or illegally, is a welcome deterrent to block the "undesirables" from entering the United States. Many will write off their veiled racism as "implicit bias," which, according to *Stanford University Encyclopedia of Philosophy*, "suggests that people can act on the basis of prejudice and stereotypes without intending to." In short, ignorance excuses bad behavior.

People tend to be more critical and incensed when hypocritical acts appear to violate their personal moral convictions. For instance, when a religious leader denounces rap music, and is discovered listening to Snoop Dogg, this form of hypocrisy may be overlooked because it doesn't register high on the morality scale. If that same religious leader condemns homosexuality and denounces gay rights, then is later discovered to engage in the same, people are more likely to be enraged. When hypocritical acts are committed by someone we don't like, we tend to be extra harsh in our judgement. For instance, when a politician that we oppose promotes family values, and is caught having an affair, he should be run out of office. When that same act is committed by someone we like, we tend to dismiss it as "tabloid trash," or to use the phrase du jour, "fake news."

THE HYPOCRISY OF CONSCIENCE

Nicholas Humphrey (2011), a leading figure in consciousness research, says consciousness is like a magic show that we stage inside our heads. This *show* is like an act that allows us to become aware of ourselves, and our surroundings. Our conscience can be hypocritical because it's constantly under threat by numerous outside temptations that assault our personal values, paving the way for self-deception. Many leaders are derailed as a result of these outside temptations. The business world encourages hypocrisy. It rewards outward evidence of inner convictions, while simultaneously rewarding outward evidence of immorality and hypocrisy. Everyone knows someone who was promoted or rewarded based on moral acts that align to the company values. Similarly, everyone knows someone who was rewarded based on indecent or improper acts. But the temptations that assault our conscience are resistible; people can't bribe their own conscience.

2

AUTHENTIC LEADERSHIP

"Authentic leadership is revealed in the alignment of what you think, what you say, and what you do."

- Michael Holland

People don't leave bad jobs, they leave bad bosses. In other words, they leave people who treat them poorly, not companies or specific responsibilities. If that sounds almost cliché, it's because it happens every day. A high performing employee resigns, and during the exit interview, the employee reveals that the manager was the root cause of their departure. According to a 2019 study conducted by Randstad, sixty percent of employees have left their jobs, or are considering leaving, because of bad bosses.

Employees see their company through their immediate leader. When leaders are hypocritical, toxic, or otherwise ill-suited to lead others, they create an atmosphere of fear, distrust, and anxiety. Conversely, when they lead authentically, employees feel inspired and engaged. Put another way, the boss is the lens through which employees view nearly everything about the company, including their relationship to it. And how employees view the company provides valuable insights into the company culture.

WHAT IS AUTHENTIC LEADERSHIP?

Authenticity isn't a quality that can be worn like a hat – put on and discarded as and when it suits us. Researchers are at pains to stress that authenticity derives from self-reflection, and from a conscious effort to align our internal values with our actions. These are gradual processes that develop over our lifetimes, and which never stop developing. Authenticity is learned, repeated, and re-assessed, which is why authentic leaders typically possess a degree of self-doubt; they are continually scrutinizing and assessing their values and actions.

Because the ability to self-reflect is essential to authenticity, an authentic person will only strive towards leadership if they strongly believe in their ability to produce positive change. Due to their strong self-belief, authentic leaders exude confidence, optimism, hope, and resilience, and actively seek ways of inspiring these qualities in their followers. Of course, as we saw in chapter 1, leaders who display these qualities are not necessarily authentic; without self-reflection and self-belief, displays of positive leadership traits are meaningless, and will likely ring false with followers.

Building on the work of researchers Shamir and Eilam (2005), Avoloi and Gardner (2005) identify four key qualities to authentic leadership:

1. Authentic leaders are true to themselves (rather than conforming to the expectations of others).

2. They are motivated by personal convictions rather than personal gain.

3. They lead from their own personal point of view, rather than seeking to reproduce pre-existing models of leadership.

4. Their actions are based on their personal values and convictions, which are built and developed through a positive moral framework.

While the key points outlined by Avolio and Gardner agree in most cases with those put forward by Shamir and Eilam, they differ in their conviction that values must be informed by ethical considerations if they are to qualify as authentic. In other words, they argue that the content of a leader's values is equally important as their ability to align their values with their actions. Without a positive moral framework, purportedly "authentic" leadership can take on ugly shapes, whereby immoral values are actualized and justified through the lens of genuine self-belief.

AUTHENTICITY AND ETHICS

Many leaders think of themselves as authentic, and they publicly profess to be so. But some leaders who profess to be authentic are delusional, and they adopt a loose definition of authentic leadership. According to Dictionary.com, "authentic" is defined as "representing one's true nature or beliefs." Loosely interpreted, this definition applies to most people who exhibit their true selves, but authentic leaders must also be ethical. If being your true self were the only test for authentic leadership, one could argue that Hitler was an authentic leader. He was certainly true to himself, and he understood the values that drove his decisions. But few could argue that his actions were ethical.

Swedish environmental activist Greta Thunberg is an example of a leader whose authenticity stems from ethical concerns. Her willingness to speak unwelcome truths to the public and to world leaders about environmental complacency has garnered her a wealth of support across the globe. Though Thunberg does not actively seek approval, her method of calmly and consistently calling out hypocrisy in politicians and corporate giants has connected with the emotions of her audience, many of whom are weary of being deceived by their leaders. In contrast to hypocritical leaders, who typically have an inflated sense of their own importance and influence, Thunberg repeatedly tells her audience, "I don't want you to listen to me, I want you to listen to the scientists." She further reprimands her audience – especially those in positions of power – for holding her up as a beacon of hope. "I don't want your hope," she tells them, "I want you to act." As will be discussed further in chapter 12, actions certainly speak louder than words, and leaders who bleat their values without acting on them risk exposing themselves as weak and hypocritical.

Though by no means a conventional leader, Thunberg's ability to rally millions of people to her cause and push for action on climate change stems precisely from her authenticity. In a society that routinely rewards lying, truthful discourses are prone to being drowned out by the sheer amount of misinformation, fake news, and outright lying that plagues our media and political rhetoric. While there will always be those who prefer a lie to an unwelcome truth, Thunberg has demonstrated that there is a taste for direct, "no-frills" honesty among the public, particularly among younger audiences who rightly view themselves as having been failed by their so-called "elders and betters."

THE PILLAR OF COMPANY CULTURE

Every company has its own unique social and psychological environment that is shaped by the values and behaviors which collectively formulate the culture of the company. The culture is something that is pre-existing in the company's genetic code. Even a sole proprietorship with no employees has a distinct culture. The values and behaviors of the owner becomes the company culture. Similarly, in larger organizations, the values and behaviors of the leaders has a deep impact on the company culture. The behavior of employees, especially those in leadership positions, and the meaning that employees attach to those behaviors ultimately shapes the company culture.

Employee perceptions of the company culture are shaped by their everyday experiences in the workplace. Since leaders are responsible for establishing the social structures of the organization, they play a vital role in ensuring that all employees align to the established culture. The actions and behaviors of leaders are constantly observed and mimicked by employees. When employees sense that leaders boldly and decisively defend the stated values and behaviors of the company, a positive and engaging culture emerges.

Delta Airlines, for instance, took bold and decisive action when they cut ties with the National Rifle Association (NRA) for their "divisive rhetoric" stemming from the shootings that took place at Marjory Stoneman Douglas High School in Parkland, Florida in 2018, killing seventeen people. Ed Bastian, the CEO, told a reporter from Inc. magazine (Schwantes, 2018), "at Delta, our values are everything. It's the culture of the company. It allows us to be who we are." In fierce defense of his company values, Bastian stated, "I really know the heartbeat of our company, and when you see something that is so polar opposite to what you believe you're required to speak, and our employees expect us to speak." The resolute action taken by Delta Airlines stands as a good example of an authentic, and socially responsible company. Bastian's decision to disassociate from the NRA met with much criticism, but the company chose values over politics.

Conversely, consider the "culture of fear and self-dealing" at the world's largest Christian college, Liberty University. The university's president, Jerry Falwell, Jr., a prominent evangelical leader and devout supporter of President Trump, has come under immense pressure for his "self-dealings" using university resources (Ambrosini, 2019). Trump's former personal attorney, Michael Cohen, alleged that he "helped clean up a lot of improper photographs" of the university president. According to over a dozen interviews conducted by Brandon Ambrosino at Politico Magazine, former confidants of Falwell reported how Falwell and his wife consolidated power at Liberty University, and directed university resources into projects and real estate deals that provided substantial financial gains for Falwell and his cronies.

TRANSPARENT LEADERSHIP

Leaders who consistently demonstrate hypocritical tendencies can't be a trusted friend, respected parent, credible role model, or an effective and revered leader if they're living a lie. As the saying goes, "some people are like pennies, two-faced and worthless." Authentic leaders, on the other hand, are genuine. They exude confidence in their beliefs, even when it's unpopular. Authentic leaders are true to their principles, they own their actions, they don't fear what others think, what others might say, or those that challenge or reject their views. They listen to, and follow, their conscience. They remain true to their followers, and most importantly, they're true to themselves, at any cost. Sadly, such leaders are rare these days. Hypocrisy among religious, civic, and business leaders has become the norm.

Lack of authentic leadership derives, at least in part, from short-sightedness, whereby the immediate benefits of deceitful behavior appeal to leaders who fail to see the long-term benefits of healthy, transparent discourses with their followers and peers. Hypocritical leaders seek to appeal to the broadest possible audience, or to the audience they believe will be of the most immediate benefit to them. While this may seem like the easier route to success, hypocrisy, once exposed, often results in loss of trust, sometimes with disastrous consequences.

Take, for example, the wide-spread mistrust, misinformation, and hypocrisy that has characterized many responses to the COVID-19 crisis across the globe. In countries such as the U.K., low-paid employees who couldn't work from home were angered by the shutting down of shops and other public venues, which had robbed them of the ability to work. Meanwhile, those who were forced to return to the workplace were incensed by the hypocrisy of their managers, who barked orders from the comfort of their own homes. The easing of lockdown measures had also met with resistance by those who accused their governments of prioritizing the economy over public health.

Far from being the result of a confused, contradictory general public, these reactions arose from communication failures and lack of trust in the motives and capabilities of political leaders. This endemic lack of trust was exacerbated by the exposure of world leaders and politicians who failed to play by their own rules, resulting in numerous scandals and public backlashes. The contradictory guidance and behavior that had plagued responses to the pandemic resulted not only in widespread criticism and resentment, but also in the spread of the virus, since some people are generally unwilling to obey rules that their own leaders openly flout.

Conversely, Jacinda Ardern, Prime Minister of New Zealand, was widely praised for securing the trust and support of her people with her swift, decisive, and transparent handling of the pandemic. By treating the virus seriously from the beginning and implementing science-based measures designed to rapidly prevent transmission, Ardern succeeded in safe-guarding public health while minimizing economic damage. She was commended for her empathetic leadership and effective communication, which played a pivotal role in securing public confidence in, and compliance with, the proposed lockdown measures (Baker, Wilson, and Anglemyer, 2020). With a landslide victory in the 2020 elections, Ardern is an excellent example of a leader who successfully aligned her values, ethics, and actions with the needs of the people she governs.

In addition to being guided by their own principals, authentic leaders listen to those who follow them, and provide opportunities for their leadership to be scrutinized. The larger the company, the more imperative it becomes to ensure that effective, transparent communication is implemented and dispersed through the entire workforce. Listening to employees and ensuring that their concerns and ideas are communicated to higher management ensures that authentic relationships are developed at all organizational levels, producing a positive, dynamic culture beyond the core leadership. Of course, doing this authentically means acting on the issues raised, rather than listening to them with no intention of taking action. If you can show employees and customers that you have listened to and acted on their feedback, trust and loyalty will likely follow.

However, offering employees the opportunity to express their concerns and ideas means nothing if the workplace culture is toxic or lax. In the former instance, employees will not speak up if they feel their contributions will be ignored or, at worst, result in punishment, such as bullying, discrimination, or even job-loss. In the case of a lax, unproductive culture, employees are unlikely to be motivated to voice their ideas, as they are simply not interested in improving the company or their own job performance. Creating and maintaining a positive workplace culture that aligns with company values is crucial if employees are to be meaningfully involved in authentic decision making. Without knowing what their workers are thinking or experiencing, leaders invite a whole host of unwelcome outcomes, from low productivity and loss of earnings to lawsuits and public shaming. Authentic leadership may seem like the more challenging route to building a successful business, but it is the only sustainable way forward.

AUTHENTIC FOLLOWSHIP

Researchers have been quick to point out that developing authentic corporate cultures depends as much on authentic followers as on authentic leaders. Working with someone whose values align with our own produces relational authenticity, whereby "leaders and followers establish open, transparent, trusting and genuine relationships" (Avolio and Gardner, 2005, p.322). Furthermore, while authentic leaders may not actively seek to inspire personal growth in their employees, this can be an organic outcome of authentic leadership, whereby employees reach higher levels of self-reflection and, therefore, authenticity, in their own conduct.

The idea of relational authenticity is certainly attractive, since it does not rely exclusively on the moral fiber and capabilities of one individual. Yet how easy is this to achieve in reality? As prospective employees, our authentic agency depends on our ability to connect our values with those of a company who represents and implements those values. However, the ability to pick and choose between companies is a privilege – something born out of the quality of our education, prior work experience, and financial stability. Those who lack formal qualifications are faced with far fewer choices, while financial pressures push many people towards taking whatever work they can get. This is disturbing, as it suggests that our capacity to make authentic decisions (i.e., to align ourselves with like-minded leaders who represent our values) is swayed largely by privilege and education. As such, when it comes to developing authentic corporate cultures, the process must begin with leaders, whose influence shapes the character of organizations and the people who work for them.

3

THE VALUE OF VALUES

*"It's not hard to make decisions
when you know what your values are."*

- Roy Disney

THE CULTURE OF AMERICA IS SHAPED BY VALUES, or ideas about what society believes to be good, right, desirable, and acceptable behaviors. Our values form the basic underpinnings for ideas of individual freedom, democracy, truth, justice, honesty, loyalty, social obligation, appropriate roles for men, women, and children, and so on. Values are not just a set of abstract ideas that guide human behavior; they are invested with considerable emotional intent. People argue, fight, and even die over values such as freedom and religion.

As individuals, we acquire our values, beliefs, attitudes, and goals through an all-encompassing process called socialization, which is a continuous process whereby individuals acquire a personal identity, and learn the norms, values, behavior, and social skills appropriate for their respective environments. Through socialization, most individuals acquire a vision, or an ultimate goal that articulates what we want to be "when we grow up." This vision is generally formed *after* we have established a personal value system, and our personal goals are generally informed by our value system. But unlike individuals, companies formulate values, or guiding principles, *after* the vision has been articulated. This reverse order makes it especially challenging for organizational members, at all levels, to align to the company values.

Every organization, large and small, begins with a vision for the future. Whether written, or unwritten, the vision is a vivid mental image that reflects the founder's aspirational goals for the organization. But a company vision reveals only the *what* of the organization. It articulates the lofty, fantastical wish of the company. *How* a company intends to pursue the vision is expressed in the form of core values, principles, or norms that form the essence of a company's identity and workplace culture. These values educate customers, potential customers, investors, suppliers, employees, and potential employees about the "personality" of the company, and the values that will be demonstrated in pursuit of the vision. An organization's commitment to the vision is expressed through an observable alignment of attitudes, behaviors, and actions of all employees to the core values of the company.

Most company values read like noble proclamations, worthy of being embraced by all employees. But the willingness to embrace company values is more challenging than one might think, because personal values and company values are not always aligned, and not all personal values are ethical. Values and ethics overlap in the sense that values are underlying core beliefs that influence the decisions we make. Ethics are different, they establish the rules for acceptable behavior. Values are only ethical when they are governed by acceptable behavior. For instance, an aspiring leader may value having power, fame, and wealth, but that doesn't mean these values are ethical. If these goals are achieved by lying, cheating, deceiving, and stealing, we can say that the values are unethical.

EMPLOYEE CYNICISM

There is much well-deserved cynicism when it comes to corporate values. In fact, they earned the dubious distinction of ranking high on a list of the most annoying, pretentious, and useless business jargon in a 2012 Forbes Magazine article. The authors of the list declared "corporate values are so phony, it churns the stomach" (Mallet *et al*, 2012). Apparently, the pessimism regarding corporate values is shared among America's workforce. According to a 2016 Gallup survey, only 23% of U.S. workers feel they can apply their company's values to their work every day, and only 27% strongly agree that they "believe in" their company's values (Dvorak and Nelson, 2016).

These findings should be alarming to business leaders because they raise fundamental questions about the level of discretionary effort that employees are willing to extend toward accomplishing their performance goals. Generally, if employees don't actually believe in their company's values, they are not motivated to contribute their personal best. The Gallup findings also reveal a massive gap between the desired culture – the one that leaders envision – and the real culture that employees experience. Too often, top leaders engage in the rigorous process of identifying a set of values designed to shape the workplace culture they aspire to create, but the values fail to resonate with the employees.

The cynicism among U.S. employees regarding their company values also reveals a lack of trust in leadership. In fact, just one in three employees in Gallup's global database strongly agree that they trust the leadership of their organization. According to Gallup, the underlying reason why most U.S. employees don't believe in their company values is that leaders only pay "lip service" to the values they trumpet. In other words, many leaders fail to align their personal values, attitudes, and behaviors to the values of the organization. Whenever employees sense a misalignment between the actions and behaviors of their leaders, and the company values, the level of trust, loyalty, and performance invariably declines.

LEADERS AS FALLING STARS

Anyone who has ever seen a shooting star can probably attest to the thrill of gazing into the sky on a cool, dark night to watch the amazing streaks of light caused by tiny bits of dust and rock falling into the Earth's atmosphere and burning up. The action of a shooting star lasts only for a few seconds. In the blink of an eye, the meteor descends, burns, then disappears, never to be seen again.

Some leaders, like falling stars, amaze their followers during the early stages. They shine brightly for a brief moment. They go fast and hard for a brief moment, and they align to the constellation, or core values of the organization for a brief moment. But many of these "shining stars" lose their sparkle over time. They gradually stray from the core values. They swap their moral compass for some sort of personal gain. Their honesty and integrity disintegrate into hypocrisy, essentially hijacking the company values.

Since leaders play such a key role in setting the moral tone for the organization, one falling star among the leadership ranks can send the organization spiraling out of control. Employees look to their leaders to demonstrate and reinforce the core values of the organization. When leaders fall out of alignment, employees are likely to mimic the destructive behavior. If gone unchecked, the behaviors that counter the core values will infect the entire organization, reshaping the workplace culture in unintended and irreversible ways.

THE NORTH STAR AS A METAPHOR

Long before GPS, travelers and explorers have relied on Polaris, the famous North Star, for a sense of direction. The unique position and visibility of the North Star, which sits almost directly above the North Pole, allows us to determine our fixed position in a spinning world, and it provides a reliable sense of direction toward the North, at least until the earth's axis changes over time, causing the stars to move in relation to each other.

The business world has adopted the North Star as a metaphor to represent a company's unwavering commitment to its vision, mission, core values, and mainly, its customers. A company's North Star leads the organization toward its vision and helps employees to stay laser-focused on the workplace behaviors that align to the core values, almost like a moral compass. The degree to which leaders and employees find their "true north" and commit to demonstrating the values, principles, and behaviors necessary to achieve the company vision, ultimately determines how effectively a company delivers on its promises to customers, and the brand image.

Every business goal, strategy, and interaction should "steer" the organization in the direction of the North Star. The core values and guiding principles of an organization define specific behaviors and actions necessary to achieve a collaborative, results-oriented workplace, and the desired customer experience. In other words, the core values are the backbone of the company vision, the essence of the company's identity. Like the North Star, core values are a constant and reliable source that helps leaders and employees to regulate their actions and behaviors. Establishing and adhering to the core values provides major advantages to the organization, both internal and external:

- **Moral Compass** – Core values provide a moral direction to guide the actions and behaviors of employees, especially in difficult times. In a volatile world of rapid technological, environmental, and societal changes, it's a much-needed constant.

- **Building Blocks** – Core values play an extremely important role in shaping a collaborative and engaging company culture.

- **Decision Making** – Core values provide a framework for making decisions that align to the company vision. For instance, if mutual respect is a core value, any disrespectful encounters among employees will be quickly and decisively resolved.

- **Customer and Employee Education** – Core values educate customers, potential customers, employees, and potential employees about the values and behaviors the organization expects to demonstrate. In this new world of social consciousness, aligning workplace behaviors to core values can be a real competitive advantage.

- **Hiring Criteria** – Core values can help managers to recruit new employees based on desirable behavioral characteristics that align to the company values.

PERSONAL VALUES MATTER

Like organizations, most leaders have a set of personal values, or core beliefs and principles, that guide us in our personal and professional lives. These values can be defined as the behaviors that you believe are most important to achieving your goals. They also help you determine how you intend to achieve your goals, what type of leader you want to be, and what actions to take as you perform your daily duties. Having a strong set of personal values as a leader helps to build trust and respect among your team, and it creates the foundation for you to influence each member in a positive way that encourages high performance and the pursuit of excellence.

Personal values help to determine the degree of "fit" with the organization, and this is true for leaders, as well as employees.

As part of the organization's governance body, leaders should screen job candidates for personal values that align to those of the organization. As "culture cops," leaders should stress ethical behavior in all workplace interactions. Since hypocrisy is so prevalent in the business discourse, the challenge for leaders is to remain authentic, which requires a strict adherence to their own personal values, and the values of the organization, while resisting the inevitable temptations to stray off course. Follow the North Star with a dogged determination to lead by example, while staying true to yourself and those you are responsible for leading, motivating, and developing into loyal employees, high performers, and brand ambassadors.

4

POLITICAL CORRECTNESS AT WORK

"Political correctness' is a label the privileged often use to distract from their privilege and hate."

- DaShanne Stokes

*I*N THE BLINK OF AN EYE, THE BACKLASH AGAINST SIMPLE CIVIL DISCOURSE BEGAN. This "simple civil discourse" is the battle cry of those advocating for political correctness, a term that has become so wildly popular, and controversial, that it now rivals the personal computer for ownership of the acronym, "PC". The phrase is so politically charged, that it has become the hot button issue of our political and social landscape, and the term has been stirring the public's emotions for decades now.

Not long ago, the popular TV show, *Politically Incorrect*, garnered the attention of the general public for nearly a decade. The host of the show, Bill Maher, rose to fame by shamelessly promoting his unwillingness to accept the social norms of civility in public discourse. He also challenged his panel of guests to do the same, often exposing their discomfort with crossing cultural boundaries. Similarly, the incendiary humor of the popular TV show, *South Park*, has pushed the limits of civil discourse to new levels. Apparently, the goal of the show, which has been airing since 1997, is to offend as many people as possible.

THE POLITICS OF "PC"

By 2016, the term "political correctness" had become the target of virtually every conservative politician in America. Donald Trump took the "anti-PC" movement to a whole new level when he campaigned for the 2016 presidential election. The self-proclaimed billionaire consistently levied a one-two punch in his speeches. On the one hand, he would utter something outrageously offensive, then pose as the brave rebel against political correctness. In fact, Trump branded himself as the "anti-PC" candidate during the GOP Presidential Debate in 2015. Trump appears to have won the presidency by leading the charge against political correctness, while simultaneously spewing what many would regard as some of the most foul, offensive, and hate-filled language. He "progressed" from dog whistling bigoted language to his base to openly hurling racist insults and threats at his rallies. Examples of Trump's anti-

PC rhetoric were widely reported around his 2016 election (Cillizza 2019), and have since formed the focus of academic research into modern politics (e.g. Finley and Esposito, 2019).

Political correctness, and its adversary, political incorrectness, have taken a stranglehold on our political and social structures, and there seems to be an insatiable appetite for, and against, the notion of civil discourse in our society. Nowhere is the PC culture more evident than in the American workplace, where unspoken rules of engagement govern virtually every interaction. This includes interactions among people of different genders, races, religions, and other highly charged social identity groups. While many in the workplace embrace the commitment to equity that underlies the PC movement, they are miffed by the barriers it conceivably creates to developing constructive, engaged dialogue in the workplace.

Another arena where political correctness appears to have overtaken common sense is the college campus, so much so that its purveyors have invented a new offense and word, the microaggression. *Merriam-Webster* defines it as, "a comment or action that subtly and often unconsciously or unintentionally expresses a prejudiced attitude toward a member of a marginalized group (such as a racial minority)." And the concept has flowed from the quad to the cubicle, as demonstrated by a 2020 article in the "Harvard Business Review," entitled "When and how to respond to Microaggressions."

"PC" AND THE "ISM'S"

In this postmodern society, businesses, organizations, and individuals are called out if they discriminate against people based on their race, religion, gender, or affectional orientation. Nowadays, employers are forced to be more sensitive to the needs and emotions of employees, and steps are taken to maintain strict adherence to these legal mandates. But despite burgeoning demands for full compliance to the PC edict, there is still relatively widespread practice of the "ism's" in the workplace. This includes racism, sexism, classism, agism, heterosexism, anti-Semitism, ableism, and other "ism's."

An African American man who is passed over for promotion often wonders whether race had anything to do with it. But he's reluctant to raise his concern out of fear of being accused of playing the "race card." A woman who earns twenty-five percent less than her male counterpart for the same job wonders whether gender plays a role. But she is loath to speak up out of fear of being labeled too "aggressive." Similarly, when a trans-gender person is purposely and repeatedly called by a name, or referred to as a different gender that they no longer identify with, many are reluctant to speak out for fear of being labeled "overly sensitive."

Political incorrectness and the ism's involve negative prejudgment of others, for the sole purpose of maintaining power and control over those who are deemed inferior. Each of these social phenomena has the ability to control and oppress others, and to establish a defined norm, or standard of rightness under which everyone is judged. In the workplace setting, this defined norm is often backed by the full powers of leadership, which makes the oppression possible and keeps it in place. In a very real sense, the ism's cannot exist without power. For example, a poor, homeless vagrant cannot really practice sexism because he lacks the means to influence the outcomes of those more fortunate than him. He has no authority or resources, so no one will notice his ill intentions.

HYPROCISY IN CULTURE MANIFESTOS

Some of the most egregious violations of political correctness have occurred in organizations that produce the most elaborate, well-written visions, mission statements, codes of conduct, and other documents designed to ensure ethical business practices. These documents often make bold declarations about honesty, integrity, equality, fairness, mutual respect, and the like. When improper acts are committed by company personnel, company executives are often called before media outlets to account for the misdeeds.

In 2019, Facebook's VP of Product Policy and Counterterrorism, Monika Bickert, appeared on Anderson Cooper 360° (CNN Business, 2019). The company was being vilified for promoting a fake video of an apparently drunk Nancy Pelosi. Many viewers failed to notice the disclaimer that identified the content as untrustworthy. In an attempt to gloss over the issue, Bickert stated, "our job is to make sure we are getting accurate information to our subscribers." But despite this noble proclamation, the company still published the untrustworthy content, garnering millions of views, and helping the company to profit from fake content.

And yet, Facebook's mission statement is to "give people the power to build community and bring the world closer together." The notion of "bringing the world closer together" was undermined when Facebook decided to permit the publishing of such offensive, incendiary, and fake content on their platform, fueling the divide among the so-called political "left" and "right." And although Facebook claims to protect their subscribers from fake content, their actions helped to turn up the heat in the political discourse.

Case in point: Facebook was widely condemned for publishing ads and memes from Russian organizations, whose goal was to confuse American voters and sow discord (Isaac and Shane, 2017), an action that hardly comports with their mission statement. In short, it's not about politics, but rather the hypocrisy that has been exposed in some of America's most prominent organizations.

The culture manifesto serves as the ideological compass of the company, and they allow employees to call out "BS" when they see it. The most powerful application of this principle is observing the reactions of leaders when someone violates the basic tenets of the documents. Does leadership take the necessary actions to mitigate the violation, or to reprimand the offender? Or do they bury their heads in the sand until the wind blows over? The answer may depend on one's position within the organization. Lower-level employees are far more likely to be reprimanded than the upper-level leaders who wield all the power.

IS "PC" THE WAY FORWARD?

The mere fact that some companies are publicly embracing the PC culture is not enough to ensure a healthy work environment for all. Some companies are tapping into the culture of diversity and tolerance. Even today, despite its prevalence, harassment in the workplace is rarely reported. This is because companies that otherwise claim to be champions of diversity take little to no action to mitigate complaints as they arise.

In the fall of 2017, the media began widespread reporting on sexual harassment and assault allegations against powerful men in the entertainment industry, which spawned the much celebrated

#MeToo movement. Heartened supporters of the movement believed that bringing these issues to the forefront would once and for all expose and punish those responsible for the assault and abuse of women. In fact, many felt that the exposure, and humiliation of the rich and powerful would deter others from engaging in such unsavory acts. Although the #MeToo movement paved the way for scores of prominent executives and movie moguls to be brought to justice, many suspect there are unintended consequences of the #MeToo movement. One example is what many felt was the unfair character assassination and subsequent resignation of Senator Al Franken, following several accusations of sexual misconduct (Mayer, 2019). And then there is Vice President Mike Pence, who famously refuses to have dinner with a female other than his wife. And now, scores of businessmen around the country have followed his lead. However, far from avoiding accusations of sexism or inappropriate conduct, Franken's attempts to publicly distance himself from women has been met with precisely these sorts of responses by those who point out the inherent sexism of refusing to dine with a colleague because of their gender (e.g. Valenti, 2017).

According to a study published in the journal, Organizational Dynamics, the #MeToo movement has resulted in a considerable reluctance among men to interact with female colleagues in the workplace. The key highlights from the study include:

- 27% of men are terrified to be alone in a room with a female co-worker.
- 21% of men would be reluctant to hire a woman for a job that requires close interaction, such as business travel.
- 19% of men would be reluctant to hire an attractive woman.

- 10% of women said they are less likely to hire an attractive woman than before the #MeToo movement.

The results of this study, and many others, suggest there is a substantial backlash to the #MeToo movement in the American workplace. A similar study previewed in the Harvard Business Review in 2019 revealed similar findings. The article headline, "The #MeToo Backlash," has become a common phrase, and it suggests that the #MeToo movement may have gone too far. Which, sadly, is another case of blaming the victim.

While the statistics quoted above show that the majority of employers are not inclined to engage in discriminatory behavior in the wake of backlashes to popular movements, these figures are nevertheless disturbing, suggesting that around a fifth of male employers have adopted negative attitudes towards female coworkers and prospective employees. It is crucial that leaders are aware of shifts in mood within their workforce in the midst of these sorts of movements, and that they are prepared to reinforce their commitment to equality through their actions. More than being an ethical obligation, maintaining equality in hiring practices is a legal obligation, and employers who flaunt their own guidance on such matters do so at their own peril.

5

HYPOCRISY IN THE WOKE CULTURE

"Don't believe everything you hear, real eyes realize real lies."

- Tupac Shakur

THERE IS MORE TALK OF DIVERSITY AND INCLUSIVITY IN WORKPLACES around the globe as companies try to reshape their work environment to demonstrate a sensitivity, awareness, and tolerance for differences and social consciousness. In other words, businesses want to show they are "woke." Merriam-Webster defines "woke" in the context of popular slang as being "aware of and actively attentive to important facts and issues (especially issues of racial and social justice)."

To be overtly woke is a great way for companies to attract new talent and new customers, especially those of the millennial generation. Naturally, everyone wants to be associated with an organization that delivers on its promise of equity and fairness. Conversely, companies that fail to deliver on this promise are often called out by current and former employees on social media outlets such as Facebook, Twitter, Reddit and Glassdoor.

Many companies attempt to broaden their appeal by catering to the new woke culture. In 2019, UK retailer, Marks & Spencer, launched a new "LGBT" sandwich, which consists of Lettuce, Guacamole, Bacon, and Tomatoes. The sandwich, and the acronym, is a play to the LGBTQ community. Marks & Spencer claimed that the campaign was designed to raise money for homeless LGBTQ youth. However, some considered the campaign to be insensitive (Young, 2019). This leads to an important question: Do companies launch such campaigns for noble purposes, or are they motivated by something more nefarious, such as profit?

On the surface, there is nothing wrong with businesses entering the realm of politics. After all, businesses wield more influence in the American political system than one might think. They spend millions on lobbyists whose sole purpose is to influence legislators. They also hire public relations and advertising firms to capitalize on contemporary political and cultural viewpoints, and rising social mores. Witness, for example, Dove's Self Esteem project, positioned as "a mission to help the next generation of women realize their full potential." What could be more woke than that? But, if companies are posing as loyalists to the new woke culture, while disguising their hypocritical motives of profit and greed, perhaps they should rethink their marketing strategy.

WOKE-WASHING BY BRANDS

Many companies are raking in big profits by exploiting the culture wars. They use clever and elaborate marketing schemes to appeal to the 'woke' culture. But in their haste for short-term profits, they often fail to consider the long-term effects of their short-sightedness. When brands or companies pretend to embrace causes that appeal to the 'woke' culture, like the exploitation of labor, sub-standard wages, discrimination, and the like, they reek of hypocrisy. And the long-term effects can be costly.

In 2019, Lacoste launched an impressive campaign under the guise of protecting endangered species. The campaign introduced ten limited-edition polo shirts that did not bear the company's popular trademarked crocodile logo. Instead, each shirt featured a different endangered species. The campaign was lauded across the globe. Social media outlets were overflowing with commentary praising the company's willingness to stand up for the diminishing species on the brink of extinction. But their appeal to the woke culture was short-lived when scores of people took to social media outlets to call out the brand's hypocrisy. For a company that proudly sells "gloves made from deer leather" and "cow leather handbags," campaigns that were aimed at highlighting the plight of animals was seen by some as the epitome of hypocrisy. How could a company that profits so mightily from the slaughter of animals pose as an advocate for endangered species?

Of course, there are countless other companies that are guilty of similar hypocritical behavior. In the 1980s, when environmental activists started sounding the alarm over the climate crisis, a famous multinational oil company responded by portraying itself as a green company. This laughable claim was used by the company as a PR exercise to make sure that people continue to buy its products. With activities that were aimed at saving the planet and the wildlife, the company was able to dupe people into believing that they were good stewards of the environment. While posing as an organization aimed at protecting the environment, this company has been fined numerous times for spilling thousands of barrels of oil in the world's oceans. In many cases, the investigators attributed the spills to "negligence."

In the wake of the #MeToo movement, Gillette launched an ad that challenged toxic masculinity. Playing on its 30-year tagline, "the best a man can get," the company replaced it with "the best men can be." The ad featured images of news clips reporting on the #MeToo movement, images of sexism in films, and images depicting other hot topics. The Gillette campaign was lauded by many advocates of the #MeToo movement, but others found the ad emasculating and demeaning to men (Taylor, 2019). The Gillette campaign, like many others, attempts to appeal to the younger generation of millennials that are acutely aware of social responsibility. Add to these "woke" offenders the many major technology and clothing companies whose shiny brand images obscure the difficult working conditions of the overseas factories where their products are manufactured.

THE MILLENIAL EFFECTS ON MARKETING

American millennials are a key consumer demographic for marketers. This group makes up nearly 25% of America's total population, and they now represent the largest purchasing block in America. According to a recent study conducted by the University of Southern California, a whopping 82% of millennials regularly interact with their chosen brands on social media outlets. According to this same study, 91% of millennials are more likely to purchase from brands that are associated with a cause.

This explains why so many top brands have adjusted their marketing strategy to appeal to the social consciousness of millennials. For instance, UBER, the popular ride-sharing app capitalized on millennials' ambivalence toward owning cars. According to the same study by the University of Southern California, a mere 15% of millennials believe it's extremely important to own a car. Perhaps this speaks to their interest in protecting the environment. Similarly, the popular, and socially responsible shoe brand, TOMS, is built on the model that, for every pair of shoes purchased, they'll donate a pair to a person in need. This is an overt appeal to the millennials' desire to associate with companies that are socially responsible.

In this age of hyper-sensitivity to social issues, it would appear it is no longer enough for brands to simply sell a product. The woke culture, fueled by the millennial generation, is keenly aware of the power of advertising and marketing on society. Companies must now have a purpose, a value system, and a deeper sense of meaning beyond the profit motive. They must take a stand for some social cause. But while posturing as a socially responsible brand, corporate leaders must also be willing to make the structural changes within their organizations to align with their public persona.

6

DIVERSITY AND INCLUSION: THE MYTH

"When we listen and celebrate what is both common and different, we become wiser, more inclusive, and better as an organization."

- Pat Wadors

*T*HERE IS MUCH HYPOCRISY IN DIVERSITY AND INCLUSION INITIATIVES. The pursuit of diversity, and the aura of inclusiveness permeates our society, and the workplace. But when you lift the veil, notions of diversity and inclusion are often just an illusion. Advocates of the diversity and inclusion initiative, including individuals and organizations, are often lacking in their ability to measure up to the basic tenets of the diversity and inclusion doctrine. The goal of diversity and inclusion, after all, is to foster an environment in which everyone is treated equitably so that they can contribute fully to society, while embracing cultural differences.

But the irony is that the "inclusive" intent behind the initiative often results in the "exclusion" of others. Exhibit A: When Brandon Eich was hired as CEO for the open source Mozilla browser project, he seemed to be the perfect fit. Eich invented the JavaScript scripting language, which is now the most widely used programming language in the world. But when diversity and inclusion advocates got wind of his hiring, they rebelled. Although Eich's fitness for the role in terms of his skills and experience was beyond question, Eich was chided for making a $1,000 contribution to a political campaign, Proposition 8, a California measure that sought to define marriage as a union strictly between the opposite sex (McCullough, 2014). Although the Mozilla board knew of this donation prior to hiring Eich, diversity advocates cried foul, and Eich was later pressured into resigning.

Mozilla, a company that prides itself on its ability to balance the liberties of equality and free speech, apparently caved to the public pressure, and effectively forced Eich to resign. A statement by a spokesperson for Mozilla hints to the hypocrisy in their dismissal of Eich, "We are committed to diversity and inclusion. We have employees with a wide diversity of views. Our culture of openness extends to encouraging staff and community to share their beliefs and opinions in public." Evidently, this only applies if your opinions echo those of the dominant majority. Mozilla's efforts to posture as an inclusive organization resulted in the exclusion of Eich's ability to share his beliefs and opinions on marriage. While Eich conceded that he was unfit to be an "effective leader" at

Mozilla given the controversy surrounding his promotion, he also pointed out the company's hypocrisy in failing to abide by their own policy of inclusiveness in their treatment of him, stating that, "If Mozilla cannot continue to operate according to its principles of inclusiveness, where you can work on the mission no matter what your background or other beliefs, I think we'll probably fail," (quoted in Shankland, 2014).

The hypocrisy among the advocates of diversity and inclusion (in this instance, those who objected to Eich's appointment to CEO) lies in their unwillingness to allow Eich's silent opposition to same-sex marriage to be registered through his private donation. The early stages of any movement involves making a case that your position deserves to be represented in the discourse, so advocates plead for a "seat at the table." But as the movement gains momentum toward majority status, advocates seem to lose their dedication to other people having the same right to have their voices heard. This is often the next phase of maturity, when the adherents shift from inviting dissent and critical thinking to consolidating power and protecting their turf.

THE "GOOD OL' BOY" NETWORK

In 2020, The Institute for Diversity and Ethics in Sports gave the NFL a "B-" rating for their racial and gender hiring practices. The league received its lowest overall score in 15 years, according to the NFL. For an organization whose workforce is 70% black, according to *The Guardian* (Lawrence, 2019), this grade is closer to a fail. The rating focused on head coaching and general manager positions. At the start of the 2019 season, there were only four people of color in head coaching positions in the NFL. The Dolphins' Chris Grier became the lone minority GM when Ozzie Newsome stepped aside in the winter of 2019, and the Raiders fired their GM, Reggie Mckenzie. To date, the NFL has only had one female GM.

When we examine the culture manifesto of the NFL, we see minimal progress toward the promise of diversity and inclusiveness. For instance, the Missions and Values section of their website, nfl.com, cites, "Respect…everyone matters, everyone contributes. We embrace all people, regardless of who they are, regardless of status, title, or background. We celebrate diverse opinions and perspectives." Unfortunately, the all-white male owners, CEO's, and presidents decided that their willingness to celebrate diverse opinions and perspectives did not extend to Colin Kaepernick, the former quarterback of the San Francisco 49ers.

During a 2016 preseason game against the Green Bay Packers, Kaepernick chose to kneel, instead of stand, during the national anthem. For the record, Kaepernick's decision to kneel was his way of peacefully protesting the brutal killing and unfair treatment of blacks by the police, an experience that any "woke" African American can attest to. The killing and beating of black Americans has been widely publicized throughout the history of America. Kaepernick's silent protest enraged many on the other side of the issue, those privileged and advantaged non-minorities who have not had the pleasure of having the life of a family member snuffed out by courtesy of an overzealous and callous police officer. During a post-game interview following Kaepernick's initial protest, he replied "I am not looking for approval. I have to stand up for people that are oppressed" (quoted in Curtis, 2020). It also stands to reason that Kaepernick was not looking for or expecting the controversy that would follow. After all, since when did standing up for the oppressed become a shameful, polarizing act? Pro sports leagues are often looking for role models and causes to extol. Witness the NFL's promotion of the armed forces, featuring pre-game flag ceremonies and fighter-jet flyovers. Supporting Kaepernick's choice to kneel could have been an easy good will score for the NFL.

But Kaepernick's actions quickly drew the fury of Donald Trump and spawned a heated national debate. NFL owners and CEO's took quick and decisive action to express their displeasure, and disapproval of Kaepernick's "unpatriotic" actions (Martin and Mchendry, 2016). Kaepernick was eventually blackballed, and players who stood in support of Kaepernick risked being fined by the NFL front office. The power within the NFL is concentrated among a select group of older, while males. But of course, this collection of 100% wealthy white guys who make the decisions for the NFL are not affected by police brutality in the same way as Kaepernick, and his fellow African American players. Within the NFL, diversity and inclusion seems to exist only within the player ranks, and there are a select few within the coaching and league office ranks. But to date there is zero representation within the ranks of owner, CEO, and president.

HYPOCRISY IN THE NATIONAL ANTHEM

A national anthem is a musical composition that recalls and eulogizes the history, traditions, and struggles of the very people who are dutifully sworn to pledge their allegiance. In America, this is considered a sacred and solemn act. The placement of the right hand over the heart while posing as a loyal and grateful citizen is a longstanding and resolute tradition in America. Anything that goes against this tradition is vehemently, and even viciously, rejected. America's chosen anthem, The Star Spangled Banner, commemorates the War of 1812, when the U.S. forces, who were being bombarded by British naval forces, raised a large American Flag over Fort McHenry in Baltimore, Maryland. For some, the singing of the national anthem, and paying homage to the flag is a most sacred event, akin to a religious experience. But for others, paying homage to this song, and this flag, is a solemn reminder of a deeply racist past and present, and a system that was designed to oppress those in the minority. From the 13th Amendment mandating that a black citizen equals three-fifths of a white citizen, to Jim Crow voting laws blocking black people from voting, to real estate redlining, to outright lynching, clearly people of color have a different relationship to American history and the rituals that commemorate it.

The time-honored, unyielding rules that govern how we are expected to address the flag conveniently ignores the ugly stains of racism and slavery that are inextricably tied to the country's past, present, and future. It is not that black people aren't patriotic, but patriotism can be paradoxical. While many African Americans see themselves as part of America, they also see themselves as separate, uninvited guests. As the African American, New York Times columnist, Charles M. Blow (2017) put it, "the flag is drenched with our blood." No matter what side of the debate you're on, it's difficult for any rational, well-intentioned person to deny the "peculiar institution" of slavery that built America and enriched the powerful. As long as the institutions of sexism, ageism, racism and slavery exist, the evasive pursuit of diversity and inclusion in our society is a mere illusion.

7

TOKENISM AND THE INCLUSION ILLUSION

"D&I needs to be something that every single employee at the company has a stake in"

- Bo Young Lee

TOKENISM IS A SURROGATE FOR DIVERSITY AND INCLUSION, it's the inevitable result of half-hearted efforts by some organizations and college admissions departments to present themselves as diverse and inclusive. It's an "inclusion illusion" of sorts. Many white people may find this concept surprising, however, the demographic makeup of an organization does not necessarily make it inclusive. Yes, today's workforce and college campuses are now comprised of people of color, women, gays, lesbians, the physically challenged, and other oppressed groups, but the real catalyst for many of these changes were environmental factors such as legislation, globalization, and the changing demographics of the labor pool. So, in order for organizations to remain prosperous, they had to at least give the appearance of a welcoming and inclusive entity. In other cases, inclusivity was the price of admission, a box to be checked for companies bidding on contracts that required a certain percentage of minority representation.

LEGISLATIVE IMPACTS TO U.S. WORKFORCE

The diverse workforce that we see today in American workplaces and college campuses did not occur through sheer generosity or the inclusive mindset of those making the hiring and admissions decisions. Nor was it the natural evolution of American society growing more open-minded after World War II, with soldiers of all races coming home after fighting together for a common cause. Instead, legislative action was necessary in order to dismantle decades of systematic racist and sexist practices designed to limit opportunities for those members of the underrepresented groups that don't fit the all-white male profile. In 1961, President John F. Kennedy issued an Executive Order that compelled federal contractors to take "affirmative action" to ensure that all applicants were treated equally without regard to race, color, religion, sex, or national origin. But the true forerunner to affirmative action was a series of government programs enacted by the Roosevelt administration in the mid to late 30's. These programs included equal opportunity clauses such as "no discrimination shall be made on the basis of race, color, or creed."

The seminal legislation, The Civil Rights Act of 1964, was the catalyst for much of the shift from an all-white male workforce, toward a more inclusive and diverse workforce, paving the way for the mass entry of women and people of color. Prior to this momentous legislation, employers routinely used factors such as race and gender in their hiring decisions, resulting in a virtually all-white male workforce, excluding, of course, those subservient positions that were deemed beneath the dignity of the privileged class. But Title VII of the Civil Rights Act of 1964 changed all that on paper by barring employers, colleges, and other entities from discriminating on the basis of race and gender, much to the chagrin of the privileged class. If these organizations wanted to practice discrimination, they would have to do it behind closed doors.

Had it not been for legislative action, and the ensuing struggles among the disenfranchised to hold employers accountable to the legal mandates, one wonders if the changes to the demographic makeup of the workforce would be nearly as drastic. After all, employers and colleges weren't exactly eager to change the homogenous makeup of their workforce. While affirmative action laws were intended to redress centuries of disenfranchisement of women and people of color, additional measures were necessary if the laws were to achieve their intended purpose. Early affirmative action laws included the use of racial quotas. But opponents argued that the use of quotas resulted in reverse-discrimination. Apparently, the U.S. Supreme Court agreed in various cases, ruling that the use of quotas was unconstitutional. Today, there are roughly nine states that have banned affirmative action altogether: California (1996), Texas (1996), Washington (1998), Florida (1999),

Michigan (2006), Nebraska (2008), Arizona (2010), New Hampshire (2012), Oklahoma (2012), and Idaho (2020). By many accounts, affirmative action laws are headed toward a slow and merciless death at the hands of American conservatism, using the concept of State's Rights as the righteous cloak for state sponsored racism.

The backlash against affirmative action, and the use of quotas, reeks of hypocrisy. To be fair, it's hard for the advantaged to see through the lens of the disadvantaged. However, those who benefit from the privilege and entitlements of a system designed to their advantage tend to view their personal lot in life as the result of their own hard work and perseverance, unable to recognize the head start they had simply due to their skin color. And those who are disadvantaged? Well, to the privileged, they somehow lack the same willingness to work hard, at best, or they're simply intellectually inferior, at worst. But the backlash against the quotas that were designed to dismantle decades of racism also reeks of hypocrisy. Of course, those that objected to the use of quotas didn't sound any alarms when the quota was 100 percent white and male.

THE SHIFT IN WORKPLACE DEMOGRAPHICS

According to the Bureau of Labor Statistics, as of 2019, non-white workers make up nearly one-third of the American labor force, including 16% Hispanic, 12% African American, and 5% Asian. Women now account for 47% of the workforce. As a result of the sweeping changes in the demographic makeup of the labor pool, the average American workplace looks vastly different from that of yesteryear. In some cases, astute, forward-thinking business leaders recognized the "browning of America," and intentionally modified their recruiting practices to attract diverse talent. But in other cases, the demographic changes of the workforce was the inevitable outcome of legislative mandates and the "browning" of the labor pool.

WITHOUT INCLUSION, DIVERSITY IS A FAÇADE

People of color and women are often promoted to positions of perceived power simply as tokens who will be obedient and reserved administrators and follow orders without making any waves. These token hires are typically agreeable servants who will not rock the boat, champion change, or challenge the status quo. In other words, these hires are little more than props that are put on display to keep the government watchdogs at bay, and to masquerade before the buying public as a culturally diverse and inclusive organization. These token hires typically do not wield the power and influence that generally comes along with their fancy job title.

It is not sufficient to hire diverse candidates without giving them a "seat at the table." After all, the concept of diversity was never meant to be a numbers exercise. Instead, it was designed to level the playing field in the workplace, college campuses, and elsewhere by extending opportunities to those who have been historically disenfranchised, while pulling from their ideas and creativity for the benefit of the organization. But when organizations hire diverse candidates just to meet a specific number, without giving them an opportunity to lend their voices in the ideation and decision-making exercises of the company, this only gives the appearance of an inclusive workplace, without actually working to achieve it. Tokenism can be a perilous practice designed to pose as a diverse and inclusive organization. It can be used to disguise inaction. The notion of tokenism is not intended to be a sweeping indictment of those organizations that have managed to cultivate a diverse and inclusive workplace. In some cases, credit is due to organizations who purposefully and intentionally changed the homogenous makeup of their workforce. But those organizations that changed the makeup of their workforce, while simultaneously reserving certain privileges for a specific few, have merely achieved diversity without inclusion.

COMBATTING TOKENISM

Diversity and inclusion are key to the harmony, longevity and prosperity of organizations. In order to cultivate a harmonious workplace, three components are necessary: cultural diversity, inclusion, and equity. Diversity is achieved when you hire individuals from underrepresented groups or a variety of backgrounds such as race, socioeconomic class, nationality, ethnicity, sexual orientation, and so on. Inclusion is achieved when hires from underrepresented groups are given an opportunity to participate in decision-making and ideation exercises. Of the three, equity is the hardest to achieve, because it requires real change, action instead of lip service. Equity in the workplace means everyone receives fair treatment, fair pay, and equal access to opportunities for advancement.

Cultivating a diverse, inclusive, and equitable workplace does not naturally evolve from changing the demographic makeup of the organization. Rather, it calls for purposeful planning to effectively integrate underrepresented members into the group. Here's a short list of some actionable steps that can be taken to cultivate a diverse and inclusive workplace:

1. **Focus on Long-term Goals...Early**

   Whether it's a new startup, or an established company, it is vital for organizations to set and communicate big-picture goals that include hiring members of underrepresented groups. Don't wait until you're called out on social media for insensitivity to protected members of the "out-groups." The following quote by Sheryl Sandberg, Facebook's Chief Operating Officer, puts it succinctly, "We are building products that people with very diverse backgrounds use, and I think we all want our company makeup to reflect the makeup of the people who use our products" (quoted in Goetz, 2020). Companies that miss out on promoting diversity are destined to be at the center of some controversy that could have been avoided.

   Large, established companies such as Burger King and H&M have been guilty of posting racially offensive ads (Ellis-Peterson, 2019; Bulman, 2020). Blunders of this sort can be minimized, or even prevented, when the demographics of the decision-makers mirror the target audience. The hiring of people from diverse backgrounds shouldn't be simply a numbers exercise; rather, it should be done for the wide range of inherent benefits of cultural diversity.

2. **Be Active in the Ecosystem**

   Members from underrepresented groups should have equal opportunity to connect with more people beyond their immediate co-workers. For instance, company-sponsored industry events, panels, and other networking events provide an opportunity for organizations to showcase their cultural diversity by meaningfully engaging those members in the planning and execution of the events. Diversity is not about numbers, it's about interaction, within and beyond the walls of the organization. The promise of high engagement, high performance, and employee retention is optimized when all employees are meaningfully engaged.

3. **Diversity - From the Bottom Up**

Many diversity initiatives start from the top, complete with a vision, mission, strategy, code of conduct, and goals of the organization. And these elaborately worded documents are typically followed by awareness workshops for the rank-and-file. But by the time the message reaches those on the front lines, the message is often interpreted very differently from the original intent.

While these actions are indeed noble and necessary, they often fail to achieve the intended purpose. By the time front-line employees get involved, the diversity and inclusion initiatives are interpreted as "the new flavor of the month," or "another program that will take away from profits and my raise." Instead, leaders should adopt a bottom-up approach that focuses on the individual, while emphasizing the "WIFM", what's in it for me? A bottom-up approach helps to operationalize the high-level strategies of the organization and promotes buy-in among those most directly impacted by the initiative. Real change happens from the bottom up, one person at a time. Every person adapts to change in different ways. A bottom-up approach helps to ensure that solutions and strategies are developed to appeal to all employees.

For example, white males often feel excluded from the diversity equation. Although that's natural, it could lead to them rejecting the program out of hand, producing the opposite result of what was intended. It's important that management demonstrates to those who are not directly targeted by diversity initiatives that their issues and concerns are just as valid as the diverse population that the organization is appealing to.

8

HYPOCRISY IN HUMAN RESOURCES

"The day we start punishing people for being honest and truthful, will also be the day we will start surrounding ourselves with liars and dishonest people."

- Sanjeev Himachali

EMPLOYEES ARE CONSIDERED "ASSETS" BY MANY ORGANIZATIONS. The motto "our people are our greatest asset," or some variation of it, has become the catch phrase of the modern era. Yes, the phrase indeed sounds noble, and few can disagree on the value of human talent in organizations. No organization can sustain without the contribution of its people.

Products are designed, produced, sold, distributed, and serviced by humans. People are the single-most important component of any business. But this trite declaration of the value of employees reeks of hypocrisy, and it generates a great deal of cynicism among employees. There are two compelling reasons why viewing employees as valuable assets generates skepticism and distrust among employees. First, the idea that humans are "assets" is flatly false. Second, there is a significant "say-do" deficit as leaders *"say"* that employees are highly valued, but they seldom *"do"* the hard work that's required to truly engage their employees.

HUMANS AS ASSETS

The idea that humans are "assets" is decidedly inaccurate. People aren't assets in the sense of tangible, fixed assets that are included in the company's balance sheet, such as buildings and equipment. According to Generally Accepted Accounting Principles (GAAP), the company must control (own) the asset, the asset must have an identifiable value, and the company must be able to transfer the control of that asset. People cannot be owned, and people generally don't want to be "controlled." There is no doubt that organizations have good intentions when they make the noble declaration of humans as valuable assets, but the trouble with the phrase is that it drives a peculiar mindset wherein humans are reduced to a disposable group of owned things to be ultimately written off as they decline in value. More to the point, humans aren't "things," they're people. It's the knowledge, skills, and abilities that are the most important determinants of business success, and these attributes certainly can't be "owned" by the employer.

THE "SAY-DO" DEFICIT

The metaphor of "humans as assets" is inherently paradoxical. It can create great insights into the high value that employees bring to their work, but it can also become a distortion because the actions taken by many organizations don't actually measure up to the lip service. We don't need to look very far to find examples of managerial practices that run contrary to the notion of "employees as valuable assets." This "value" is put to the test when organizations are faced with the need to cut expenses. When leaders need to "trim the fat," where are they most likely to look first? You guessed it, the people, or shall we say, "the most valuable assets." So, instead of doing the hard work of identifying wasteful spending across the enterprise, the instinct is to send the "assets" to the unemployment rolls.

The reality is that layoffs and reductions in force are sometimes necessary. Global competition has captured a considerable share of American marketplace. With labor costs topping the list of the company's greatest expense, employees quickly become expendable when leaders need to cut costs. But expense management is effective only when it's carried out in a prudent and thoughtful manner – without sacrificing the hope and aspirations of the affected and unaffected employees. It is shocking how frequently the needs of employees, or "assets," are dismissed during the crucial work of planning cost-reduction initiatives within organizations. The result is often a suffocating bureaucracy and a micro-managed, dispirited workforce.

According to Gallup's 2016 survey on employee engagement, only 32% of employees in the U.S. are engaged – meaning they are actively participating in, enthusiastic about, and fully committed to their work. Globally, a mere 13% of employees are actively engaged. With so many organizations declaring employees are their most valuable asset, you would expect to see higher levels of engagement. But low engagement is inevitable when employees sense a misalignment between what leaders *say*, and what they actually *do*.

Ask employers why people quit their jobs, and most will tell you it's about the money. Ask employees the same question, and you're likely to get a whole different story. An enormous 2019 study conducted by employee engagement platform, Peakon, curated over eleven million survey comments to provide employers with the top desires and frustrations that cause employees to seek employment elsewhere. The findings of the Peakon study revealed the top three things that employees would most want to change about their current place of employment. Here are the key insights that ranked in the top three:

1. **Improved Communications**

    Survey respondents felt they would benefit most from improved communication. Employees simply want to be in the know. One-third of the respondents indicated that communication was severely lacking. This deficiency indicates that coaching and feedback sessions were very limited, at best, or practically non-existent, at worst.

    A related study was conducted by Dynamic Signal in 2019 among 1,000 U.S. employees. Two-thirds of the respondents considered quitting solely because of a lack of communication. With advanced technology, such as instant messaging and video chat, employers have readily available communication channels at their fingertips. Employees feel a greater sense of worth and belonging when their leaders take the time to personally engage them, and this sense of belonging translates to higher engagement, higher productivity, and ultimately lower operating costs.

2. **Improved Employee-Manager Relationships**

   The employee-manager relationship is a key factor in retaining top employees. A 2018 Udemy study found that nearly half of employees surveyed quit because of a bad relationship with their direct supervisor. Almost two-thirds believed their supervisor lacked the training and skills to be a good leader. Effective front-line supervisors and managers are the key to aligning employee performance to the goals of the organization. If leaders want to avoid the high cost of employee turnover, hiring, training, and developing effective leaders would be a great start.

3. **Improved Workplace Environment**

   The role of the work environment is arguably the most neglected and misunderstood roles of leadership. Leaders tend to view the work environment only in terms of the physical elements. The work environment is the combination of the setting, social features, and physical conditions in which employees perform their jobs. These elements shape the overall culture of the organization, and they impact workplace relationships, collaboration, efficiency, and even the health and well-being of employees.

One of the most common misconceptions that leaders hold is that they can directly motivate their employees. This idea is preposterous, and a gross overestimation of their abilities. Here's the point: humans are complex beings and there is no single, sure-fire tactic that leaders can employ that generates long-term, sustained motivation. High motivational levels result from a combination of sustained intrinsic and extrinsic factors that ultimately shape the employee's level of motivation and commitment. Simply put, effective leaders understand how to use the appropriate levers within the work environment (extrinsic) to positively influence the employee's self-worth and job satisfaction (intrinsic).

MOTIVATING AND RETAINING EMPLOYEES

Taking steps to engage your employees by offering them tangible steps to improve their performance and career prospects is key to maintaining a healthy work force. Here is a brief list of actions that organizations can carry out to retain their employees and ensure long-term growth:

1. **Trust and Responsibility**

    Many organizational leaders are hesitant when it comes to assigning increased responsibilities that are outside an employee's job description. However, leaders have both a duty and an incentive to invest in the development of their employees, since motivated, high-performing workers are immensely valuable to any company. Offering short-term special assignments or supervisory roles to those employees who have demonstrated the ability to tackle higher levels of responsibility is a good tactic that will help them to practice, and develop, their leadership skills. In the absence of challenging work and career development opportunities, employees are likely to have one foot in the workplace, and the other in the job market.

2. **Appreciation**

   High-performing employees take ownership of their work and expect managers to acknowledge their efforts. The benefits of recognizing and rewarding good work are obvious, since employees are likely to repeat performance and behaviors that are rewarded by their leaders. Lack of appreciation leads to stagnation in the workforce, not least because high-performing employees whose efforts are not recognized are more likely to search for employers who will value their skills.

3. **Guidance and Mentoring**

   Formal mentoring systems have the dual benefit of allowing high-performing employees to practice their leadership skills, while improving the skills of new or underperforming employees. A mentor is usually a more experienced coworker whose skills and knowledge can be utilized to guide less experienced colleagues. New starters in particular tend to feel more comfortable with communicating any difficulties they encounter to a mentor rather than to a supervisor or manager. The freedom to ask questions and learn from the expertise of coworkers is crucial to developing and retaining employees.

4. Learning Opportunities

   Employees seek out companies that have something to offer besides a set of routine tasks and a paycheck. Lack of opportunity breeds stagnation, which is why most employees crave more challenging activities that allow them to learn new skills and build connections within, and beyond, the industry. Training opportunities and networking events are worthwhile investments for any employer looking to attract and maintain workers.

INERTIA

Understanding why employees remain in the workplace is as important as understanding why they leave. As Flowers and Hughes (1973) point out, many organizations focus disproportionately on the causes behind their employees leaving, for example by conducting exit interviews. While this is a valuable way to identify 'push' factors within the company (i.e. internal issues that cause people to leave), this emphasis also reveals a lack of awareness about why people stay.

A common misconception among employers is that people stay because they are satisfied. However, the reasons behind inertia are more complex than this. Though job satisfaction is an important cause of inertia, there is a wide range of 'push' and 'pull' factors that lead to an employee choosing to stay put. Some of these factors are internal (related to the company), while others are external (relating to the employee's career prospects and personal life outside the company).

Job satisfaction and company environment are key factors in determining whether or not an employee chooses to remain with the company. If either of these things is weak or inadequate, employees are more likely to leave. However, leaders need to be aware that toxic environments and lack of opportunity within the organization can also result in inertia. When people lose motivation at work, this can also result in losing the motivation to leave. Most of us are familiar with the phrase "stuck in a rut," which is commonly applied to work situations. Employers have a duty and an incentive to assess whether their retention levels are a result of a positive work environment, or a disheartened workforce who lack the energy, ambition, and career opportunities to seek out something preferable.

EMPLOYEES ARE CUSTOMERS TOO

There seems to be a growing sense that employees and customers have a lot in common. If leaders were to embrace employees as "internal" customers, unequivocally and passionately, the impact to employee morale, commitment, and productivity, would be transformational. After all, the list of commonalities between employees and customers is remarkably similar. Here's a few of the most compelling similarities:

1. **Low Barriers to Switching**

    Globalization and technology have made it easier for competitors to poach your customers and employees. When customers become disenchanted with a specific brand, switching to a more desirable brand has never been easier. Similarly, when employees lose interest in their employer, alternatives are right at their fingertips.

2. **Both are Targeted for Brand Loyalty**

    Employers are interested in building brand loyalty among their customers by producing quality products and services that promote brand loyalty. Worldwide spending by companies for market research exceeded $68 billion dollars, a clear indicator of the value that leaders place on understanding evolving customer demands. Similarly, employers expect their employees to be enthusiastic brand ambassadors. But the level of effort extended by many employers to promote employee ambassadorship is severely lacking. According to Gartner, global spending by employers in Customer Relationship Management systems is 4x greater than spending in Human Capital Management systems.

3. **Changing Attitudes**

    According to the U.S. Census Bureau, millennials became the largest block in the U.S. labor force, reaching 56 million in 2016, which is roughly 48 percent of the total U.S. labor force. By the year 2030, millennials are expected to represent 75% of the total U.S. labor force. As consumers, millennials account for more than $600 billion dollars in annual spending.

Although no generation behaves exactly like the last, millennials are credited for making unprecedented changes to the American workplace and marketplace just by their sheer size. Millennials are leveraging their influence to drive sweeping changes in the marketplace, and the workplace. American companies are put on notice that social responsibility and fair treatment in the workplace are key expectations of the millennial generation. Millennials are far more deliberate when choosing where to buy their products, and which employer to work for. For them, it's more than a product. It's an aligned purpose or belief in a brand that takes social responsibility seriously. And it's more than a job, it's about organizational purpose and integrity.

In order to win in the marketplace, employers must first win in the workplace. An empowered workforce underpins any efforts to improve the customer experience. When the employee experience is optimized, the customer experience is positively impacted. And together, both outcomes improve profitability, productivity, and brand loyalty. Despite the obvious inter-dependency between employee satisfaction and customer satisfaction, many leaders are failing to meet the needs of their "most important asset," employees. Managers would do well to learn how to listen to, and understand their employees by engaging in frequent, meaningful dialogue, rather than a broad-based, one-size-fits-all approach. Like consumers, employees only pay attention to messages that are relevant to them.

9

THE UNPLEASANT CONSEQUENCES OF HYPOCRISY

"Hypocrisy is the audacity to preach integrity from a den of corruption."

- Wes Fowler

EVERY COMPANY HAS ITS OWN DISTINCT CULTURE. A company culture doesn't really take any special planning, it develops and flexes organically over time. The basic building blocks of a company's culture are usually echoed in the culture manifesto; whether it's a set of shared values, a code of conduct, or an employee handbook. Although a workplace culture develops naturally over time, the results may not be exactly what the company leaders had in mind. The most engaging company culture evolves from effective planning, and strict adherence to the norms and rules that govern employee conduct.

Similarly, every company has a strategy, which determines how a company pursues its goals. In its raw form, a strategy is any plan, method, or series of maneuvers designed to obtain a specific goal or result. The interesting thing about strategy and culture is that both develop naturally over time, without the need for company leaders to invest any time and energy to create them. But the best strategies are formally designed, rational and logical plans that outlines the methods and tactics that will be employed to achieve the company goals. Likewise, welcoming, collaborative, results-oriented workplace cultures don't just magically occur. Instead, it takes careful planning by organizational leaders.

Well-designed strategies are deliberate, coherent, and easy for employees to understand. But culture is emotional, dynamic, and vulnerable because it directly affects the morale, engagement, and performance of employees. Culture is a fickle phenomenon that generally flexes with the top leaders. One change among the top brass of an organization can result in a sweeping culture change. But strategy and culture share an interesting relationship. There is a co-dependency among the two. Strategy is the compass that drives focus and direction, while culture is the emotional, organic climate that ultimately determines whether a company's strategy lives or dies.

WHEN STRATEGY AND CULTURE ARE MISALIGNED

Many companies are run by leaders whose thinking is heavily skewed to the rational, financial, and strategy side of the equation. Meanwhile, the culture side, since it involves people, is often subordinated, misunderstood, and even dismissed altogether. When leaders overemphasize strategy, while de-emphasizing culture, this imbalance is a form of hypocrisy, and the consequences can be dire. Strategy doesn't trump culture, culture trumps strategy. But despite this somewhat obvious fact, few leaders choose to invest the time and resources into developing a coherent and cohesive culture.

When strategy and culture are misaligned, all the value statements uttered by the leaders become nothing more than window dressing, and the company culture is hijacked by the obvious hypocrisy. But what may not be so obvious is the awareness among leaders of the destructive consequences for allowing it to happen.

Employees expect their company values to be honored. When the core values and guiding principles are hijacked by the hypocrisy of the leaders, employees are left to conclude that the company doesn't mean what it says, leaders value profits over people, their work isn't valued, and behaving in ways that contradict the values is perfectly acceptable. The fallout from the misalignment between strategy and culture reeks of hypocrisy, and the impact to the company and its employees is costly.

When employees sense hypocrisy among their leaders, some may be inclined to hold their leader accountable in public forums. For instance, in February of 2020, Amazon chief, Jeff Bezos, proudly announced his intention to donate a whopping $10 billion to his new "Bezos Earth Fund," an initiative aimed at positioning Amazon as climate champions by combating global warming. But while contributing ostentatiously to this noble cause, Amazon is accused of contributing massively to carbon emissions (Ibbetson, 2020).

The dichotomy of protecting the climate through donations while simultaneously contributing to its ruin through company actions prompted a group of Amazon employees to take to social media to blast the multi-billionaire CEO for his hypocrisy. Bezos is alleged to have threatened any worker who engages in climate activism. The irony is that the alleged threats by Bezos against his outspoken employees is misaligned with one of the company's 14 Leadership Principles included in the company's website, "earn trust…listen attentively, speak candidly, and treat others respectfully."

ONE COMPANY, TWO CULTURES

The term "culture" has many definitions and interpretations across the business landscape. Gallup defines culture as "how employees interact, and how work gets done." Although many organizations claim to have engaging cultures, there is often a great disparity between the culture that leaders envision, and the culture that employees experience. Leaders can become so mired in the day-to-day grunt work that they are oblivious to the obvious signs that two cultures exist; the one that leaders envision and experience, versus the culture that employees experience on the front lines of the organization.

Whenever two cultures exist within the organization, there is also a misalignment between strategy and culture. Here's a shortlist of some of the most common negative outcomes:

1. **Damaged Reputation**

    When culture and strategy clash, the culture of the company deteriorates, and the day-to-day operations fall in sync with the declining culture, followed by diminishing product or service quality, employee disengagement, and high employee turnover. People prefer to work for a company that operates in a consistent manner, where values are aligned with strategy and culture. Likewise, customers prefer brands that are ethical, and socially responsible, and the expectations among employees and consumers are even more pronounced in today's "woke" culture.

2. **Lost Sense of Mission and Purpose**

    When strategy and culture are in sync, this creates a compass effect because it instills in the employees a sense of clarity of direction, and it guides their actions and decisions. But when culture and strategy are misaligned, employees will default to self-serving actions and behaviors. As a result, they tend to perform at the most basic levels acceptable to their leaders, and they are less willing to devote any portion of their discretionary effort to pursuing the goals of the company, and the sense of mission, purpose, and camaraderie is lost.

3. **Disoriented Employees**

   When the actions of leaders are not consistent with the company strategy, employees become disoriented, and they lack a sense of direction. In many cases, employees observe leaders' rewarding a set of behaviors that are inconsistent with the values of the organization.

4. **Increased Employee Turnover**

   Employees prefer to work for a company that operates in a manner consistent with its stated values. Virtually every company makes claims to honesty, integrity, and other noble traits in the culture manifesto. And when organizations operate in a manner consistent with these claims, this creates a strong sense of belonging, and inspires loyalty and commitment at all levels. On the other hand, when employees sense dishonesty and hypocrisy, they'll seek it elsewhere.

5. **Difficulty Attracting New Talent**

   Job seekers, especially the high caliber ones, prefer to work for companies that have a reputation for honesty, integrity, and good product or service quality. Social media platforms and enhanced technology makes it incredibly easy for job seekers to do their homework, and candidates want to know what makes a potential employer a great place to work. Today's highly competitive job market underscores the importance of leading with honesty and integrity.

Effective leadership is about more than just meeting a set of numbers or objectives. It's about creating an engaging work environment characterized by ethical behavior, truth-telling, transparency, fairness, collaboration, and alignment between the vision, values, attitudes, and behaviors of employees, at every level. Contrary to popular belief, employees are not indelibly motivated by money, trinkets, or any other carrot-and-stick tactic. The conditions in the work environment are the key determinant of employee morale and engagement. It includes everything from office décor, furniture, and computers, to the attitudes and behaviors of employees, including the leaders. The work environment is the evidence of a company's intention to treat employees fairly, respectfully, and equitably. We often hear companies such as Starbucks, Google, and Zappos praised for their outstanding corporate culture. There's a reason for this. The leaders of these companies have made the commitment to fully align their culture with their strategies. With every organizational choice they make, they reinforce that commitment. By embracing that level of dedication to alignment, any organization can conquer cultural problems to achieve stellar performance.

10

THE DARK SIDE OF "EI"

"If you are tuned out of your own emotions, you will be poor at reading them in other people"

- Daniel Goleman

EFFECTIVE LEADERS PLAY TO THE EMOTIONS OF THEIR FOLLOWERS. For good or ill, appealing to people in a way that transcends the intellectual and the rational is a hallmark of great leaders. They all have it, and they use it to engender commitment and loyalty among their followers. Most great leaders understand that once their followers are inspired, they will be inclined to offer a greater share of their discretionary effort toward meeting the goals of the organization.

One of the most effective ways successful leaders connect with their followers is through emotional intelligence (EI), a term popularized by Daniel Goleman, in his 1995 best-selling book, Emotional Intelligence. The most effective leaders use emotional intelligence in positive ways to manage their own emotions, influence others, display empathy, defuse conflict, and communicate more effectively with their followers. Leaders convey emotional intelligence by speaking directly to the needs and desires of their followers. When leaders speak to those needs, and, when possible, meet those needs, their followers feel understood, and they will generally respond in ways that demonstrate their buy-in, loyalty, and commitment.

Some of the greatest moments in human history were fueled by emotional intelligence. When Dr. Martin Luther King delivered his famous "I Have a Dream" speech to his audience of 250,000 in the 1963 March on Washington, he mesmerized his audience by uttering words that were sure to stir their hearts and emotions. "Instead of honoring this sacred obligation to liberty," King roared, "America has given the negro people a bad check!" After centuries of human enslavement in the United States, and broken promises of liberty for all, King's famous speech inspired millions, and instilled hope by enabling his audience to envision a future in which former slaves and the descendants of former slave-owners will be able to live in harmony. King inspired a mass movement that paved the way for the Civil Rights Act of 1964 and changed the world in unprecedented ways.

Tapping the emotions of followers in a way that transcends the conscious mind requires great skill. King delivered his speech by conveying a tone of pained indignation and distress that aligned perfectly with the sentiments of his audience, and he is rightfully regarded as one of the most influential leaders in the history of the world. One of his greatest strengths was his ability to appeal to his followers on an emotional level, and he used this special ability for the greater good.

DECEPTIVE USE OF EI

Emotional intelligence is not inherently virtuous; it can be used as a tool to manipulate followers to take actions that are counter to their own best interests. According to British historian, Roger Moorehouse, Adolph Hitler honed his emotional intelligence through years of studying the emotional effects of his hand gestures and body movements on his audience. Hitler reportedly practiced his hand gestures and body movements until he perfected his ability to leave his audience spellbound. Though his intentions lacked ethical convictions, Hitler recognized the power of human emotions, and he played to the natural sensitivities of his followers.

Although Hitler's use of emotional intelligence served his own nefarious personal agenda, few can argue against his ability to inspire his followers in a way that engendered loyalty and commitment. Sadly, this "dark" side of emotional intelligence is commonly practiced by organizational leaders in pursuit of their own self-interest. This "hidden agenda" is often undetected by devout followers because, once human emotions are aroused, we are less likely to think rationally and logically.

EMOTIONS CAN SUPPRESS RATIONALITY

Similar to knockoffs of luxury watches, emotions can appear authentic to unsuspecting followers. Many leaders intentionally inject emotion into their speeches for the purpose of eliciting emotional responses among their followers. This "add emotions and stir" approach to leadership plays to the natural instincts of human behavior. Once human emotions are aroused, our response is often dictated by the type of emotion experienced. When a person feels frustration, anger, tension, or fear, they are more likely to act aggressively toward others. Likewise, when a person feels joy, pride, interest, and hope, they are more likely to act in a positive manner.

Humans are born equipped with a set of predictable responses to situations. The instinct of a newborn baby is to cry. When faced with the death of a loved one, we feel a sense of sadness. This natural, emotional vulnerability of humans provides a pathway for leaders to connect with their followers, for good or ill. And the reality is that hypocritical leaders understand that human emotions are generally separate from rationality. Therefore, they appeal to the emotions of their followers knowing that rational thinking will be subconsciously discarded. The irony is that emotional intelligence teaches us to discard our emotions so that we can think more rationally and objectively, but since human emotions generally trump rationality, we're left with the binary choice of emotional subjectivity vs. rational objectivity.

Emotional intelligence is a quality that we have come to expect from successful leaders. But the unbridled enthusiasm that it engenders can be used to obscure the self-serving, and often nefarious, intentions of hypocritical leaders. The fact is, once human emotions are roused, most humans are far less likely to remain objective and rational in their thoughts and actions. And when emotions are at their highest point, some are capable of being herded like mindless sheep.

DO EMOTIONS MATTER IN THE WORKPLACE?

Jochen Menges, a renowned researcher at the University of Cambridge, has done extensive studies on the effects of emotions on organizational behavior. Menges was particularly interested in studying the causes and effects of the various "moods" of organizations. Menges' studies (e.g. Menges, Kilduff, Kern, and Bruch, 2015), involving roughly 20,000 employees across 100 organizations, examined the effects of various leadership styles on the emotional climate of organizations. What he found was that the people at the top had a profound effect on the emotional state of the employees. Some companies had an atmosphere of "dynamism," while others had an atmosphere of fear and "defeatism." Menges' research revealed that charismatic leaders can have both positive and negative outcomes. On the positive side, employees can be inspired by charismatic leaders. But on the negative side, employees can be so "awe-struck" by their leader that their cognitive abilities are severely diminished.

In a related study conducted by Menges in 2009, he was interested in analyzing the reactions of a specific group of employees to the same speech delivered by their leader. The leader was asked to deliver the speech in two different styles. The first speech was delivered with passion and emotion. Six months later, the same speech was delivered to the same group of employees, but without passion and emotion. Menges discovered that employees were able to recall the key points in the "emotion-less" speech, but unable to recall the key points in the speech delivered with emotion. Menges concluded that when people are mesmerized, they seem to lose the capacity to recall and rationalize.

The best leaders understand the great power and influence that their emotions have on the company culture. They leverage this power for the greater good of the company and their employees. Effective use of emotional intelligence plays a vital role in inspiring employees to deliver their personal best toward accomplishing their performance goals, and the goals of the organization.

But hypocritical leaders use emotional intelligence to manipulate followers for their own self-interest, betting that their followers won't bother to fact-check. This form of deceptive leadership creates a dysfunctional workplace culture that is virtually irreversible.

11

TRUTH-TELLING AIN'T EASY

"Pretty much all the honest truth-telling there is in the world is done by children."

- Oliver Wendell Holmes

*I*T'S ACTUALLY MUCH HARDER TO BE AN AUTHENTIC LEADER THAN IT APPEARS. We're living in some interesting times where it has become socially acceptable for politicians to develop their own set of "alternative facts," while dismissing anything that runs contrary to these "facts" as "fake news." There is no shortage of political commentary to be fact-checked by investigative journalists. The adage, "believe none of what you hear, and only half of what you see" no longer prevails.

Thanks to artificial intelligence, and sweeping advancements in technology, "deep fake" audio and video can hijack entire identities and deceive the public in unprecedented and convincing ways. We are experiencing a renaissance of sorts, where reality and alternative facts have become virtually indistinguishable, and it won't be long before corporate giants begin to mimic this intractable discourse.

Make a list of 5 leaders that you most admire, then ask yourself why you admire them. Chances are, the reasons you admire them so much is based more on how they connect with you emotionally, than on their accomplishments or their ability to deliver on promises made. This is because humans are emotional beings, and we tend to follow leaders who appeal more to our emotions than our conscience. As emotional beings, we are less inclined to fact-check a leader who appeals to our emotions.

Ask a group of Trump loyalists why they follow him so devoutly, and you are likely to get a wide range of responses, but truth-telling won't make the list. In many ways, some might say Trump is authentically false, rather than falsely authentic. Trump's followers take him seriously, but not literally, and most people who are not devout followers take him literally, but not seriously. Perhaps Trump's ability to connect emotionally with his followers, despite his loose relationship with the truth, reveals some unflattering truths about human nature.

Consider the wide range of promises that a typical candidate makes when running for public office. George Bush Sr's famous "Read my lips: no new taxes" phrase was exactly what voters wanted to hear in the moment, and the memorable phrase was so indelibly etched in the public conscience, that they cast their ballots in his favor, and he was sitting in the Oval Office the following January. But two years later, the emotional appeal of his slogan backfired when he signed the Omnibus Budget Reconciliation Act of 1990, increasing the individual tax rate from 28% to 31%. The one-term president appealed to the emotions of voters with a simple, memorable slogan, but failed to win his re-election bid, likely as a result of his hypocrisy. We might say that his short-term gain came at the expense of his re-election.

EVEN GOOD PEOPLE TELL LIES

There is one indisputable truth where humans are concerned, we all lie, and that's the truth! Telling your best friend that she really does look fat in those leotards is unthinkable. Or telling your wife that you really are attracted to that young, beautiful, shapely assistant you just hired might land you in divorce court. These, and other "little white lies" are used as a means of peacekeeping, and in some cases, survival. Unless you're testifying before a Grand Jury, little white lies can be harmless. But when you're answering to your stockholders or employees, the impact can be disastrous.

According to Charles Honts, a researcher and professor of psychology at Boise State University in Idaho, most humans tell lies in roughly 25 percent of their social interactions. Although the reasons vary, most lies boil down to the desire to look good to ourselves, and to others. And it turns out that humans aren't very good at "deception detection." Various studies have been conducted to test the ability of participants to distinguish between truth and lies. Observers are typically given videotaped statements from various speakers who are either lying or telling the truth. After watching the recorded video, observers are asked to judge whether the statement was true or false. According to applied social psychologist, Aldert Vrij, the average accuracy rate among participants in these various studies is around 57%. When we consider the odds of being correct are 50/50, the results aren't very good, and they reveal the natural vulnerabilities of humans. Simply put, humans are easy prey for hypocritical actors.

PRACTICE MAKES PERFECT

We live in a society that rewards lies and punishes truth-telling. In a typical 10-minute conversation, the average person lies 2-3 times. That's not cynicism, that's science. We are taught to lie at a very early age. And lying has seemingly become an important developmental milestone like crawling and walking. When a parent tells their child, "no matter what, tell your aunt Kate you like the gift," the parent has every expectation that the child will follow through. And if the child chooses to defy the parent's insistence, there will likely be unpleasant consequences.

From childhood, we learn to associate specific behaviors with specific outcomes. This method of learning, referred to as "operant conditioning," is reinforced as deeds that are considered socially acceptable are rewarded, while those deeds considered unacceptable are punished. So, in order to maximize our rewards, and minimize unfavorable outcomes, such as punishment and judgment, we've adjusted our moral compass to permit lying in certain circumstances.

CORPORATE DARWINISM

The corporate world can be cruel and ruthless. Shareholders pressure corporate leaders to maximize returns at any cost. Corporate giants lobby the federal government to pass laws that are harmful, and even deadly, to the public. Corporate officers are preoccupied with maximizing their bonuses, at any cost. The healthcare system is designed to keep people sick, instead of making them well, so they can peddle their expensive drugs. Common workers barely earn enough to keep food on the table. Corporate giants like Coke and Pepsi top the list of companies producing the most ocean pollution (McVeigh, 2020). Despite heavy scrutiny and mountains of government regulations, corporate behemoths manage to survive, while smaller, less powerful companies wither and die.

The corporate world has never been as callous as it is today. It's a dog-eat-dog world, and only the most ruthless survive. While large organizations try to put on a friendly face, there's a great deal of hypocrisy and greed that goes on behind the scenes. Amazon, the largest retailer in the world, is widely criticized for driving prices down to drive out competition (Hankin, 2019), while engaging in inhumane treatment of their employees (Lee Yohn, 2020). DowDuPont tried to lobby the White House to ignore evidence that their pesticide product line is harmful to about 1,800 endangered species (Martin, 2017). And Morgan Stanley agreed to pay a whopping $3.2 billion for its role in the subprime mortgage crisis that led to the Great Recession of 2008 (Smith, 2016). The list of deceptive practices among the largest companies on the planet is practically endless.

Lies and deception permeate our businesses, our churches, our school systems, and society in general. We live in a world where truth-telling has been so diminished in value, that the alternative often has greater appeal. But liars aren't solely to blame for the lying epidemic; our political, social, and organizational and societal norms have deteriorated to a point where truth and transparency are taboo.

MORALS FOR SALE

Leading authentically is particularly hard in large organizations, where aspiring leaders jockey for annual bonus dollars, or that next promotional opportunity. It is generally true that our actions are guided by our morals and values, but only to a certain extent. The pursuit of self-interest often gets in the way. People are quick to swap their moral values for personal gain.

A study conducted by neuroeconomists at the University of Zurich (Obeso *et al*, 2008) found that, while most people are predisposed towards supporting moral causes as opposed to harmful ones, most will eventually switch to selfish behavior if the monetary reward is high enough. Participants in the study were, however, more consistent in their moral decisions when electromagnetic stimulation was applied to the area of the brain responsible for debating the "morals versus money" conundrum. This suggests that selfish acts emerge from deliberation, and that when the brain's capacity for deliberation is subdued, our moral instincts tend to prevail. As one might expect, the study also found that people are less willing to make selfish choices when they are being watched. Few people like to be caught doing the wrong thing, which is why so many "dodgy dealings" take place behind closed doors.

If external perception subdues selfish decision making, then it follows that fear of being caught factors into our moral conduct. While the prevalence of deceitful, hypocritical behavior in corporate and political spheres indicates that being caught isn't as much of a deterrent as we might hope, increased public scrutiny is pushing for transparency in the dealings of the rich and powerful. Donald Trump, for example, has been under immense public pressure since his 2016 election to reveal his tax returns, and his repeated attempts to skirt the issue have only served to heighten suspicions of malpractice (Thomas, 2016). Indeed, the rich and powerful are rarely as subtle in their deceitful actions as they believe themselves to be, fooling themselves into forgetting that the public can smell a rat a mile away.

Employees are also becoming increasingly savvy about recognizing unscrupulous behavior within the organizations they work for. This, coupled with a greater awareness of employee rights and legal protections, has produced a growing number of emboldened workers who will resort to whistleblowing if morally dubious practices are not dealt with internally. Once malpractice is identified, it is generally difficult to sweep under the rug, especially given the power of social media to spread and amplify public shaming.

If financial incentives lead to corruption, then our faith in corporate integrity ought to be directed more towards transparent cultures than towards the moral fiber of individual leaders. Authentic leaders know this, and are generally unafraid to speak about, and defend, their values and actions in public arenas. Crucially, morality is not down to one individual; the moral character of a leader can only be weighed with external scrutiny of their actions.

That being said, leaders should not wait for someone else to point out when their moral compass shifts away from true north. As discussed above, we are so successful at deception that we are even capable of deceiving ourselves. This means that, on occasion, we may not even be aware that what we are doing is unethical. For this reason, it's essential that we check-in with ourselves now and then. If we find ourselves coming up short on our own moral values, we need to re-evaluate, and take responsibility for, our actions. The capacity to be honest with ourselves is just as important as being honest with others.

12

WHY ACTIONS MATTER MORE THAN WORDS

"Words are from the lips, actions are from the heart."

- Rashida Costa

THE WORDS OF A LEADER MAY BE HEARD, BUT ACTIONS ARE IMITATED. Like watchful adolescents, employees are constantly taking in the world around them, and they are particularly observant of the actions and behaviors of the leadership in search of clues that signal the leader's values, expectations, attitude toward employees, and so on. The conclusions that employees draw from these observations inform the employee's overall level of satisfaction and engagement. And the level of discretionary effort that employees ultimately extend toward the accomplishment of performance goals is directly tied to the work environment, and the actions of the leader. If the actions and behaviors of the leader are misaligned with the core values, employees are likely to repeat the same behaviors.

There are as many definitions of leadership as there are stars in the sky, yet the common theme about leadership is the concept of alignment. A leader's actions and behavior must align to the vision, mission, and core values of the organization. Alignment simply means "walking the talk," "put your money where your mouth is," or simply "leading by example." Aligning to the core values of the company isn't easy, because it requires us to make decisions and take actions that line up with the goals, ideas, and beliefs of the company, some of which may be in conflict.

The danger in leaders behaving poorly is that it isn't confined to the leader just being viewed in a bad light. A negative impression of a leader, especially those at the very top, extends to the employees, the business, and the brand. The leader's behavior is inarguably the most important determinant of performance results, and the collective behavior of the leadership dictates the performance capacity of the organization.

IT'S ABOUT MORE THAN BUSINESS RESULTS

Many loathsome leaders today have become delusional by pointing to strong business results as a sign of their effective leadership. They employ tactics such as "do as I say, not as I do," and "rule with an iron fist." They threaten, coerce, and even humiliate the very people they are responsible for leading, or those often referred to as "the most valuable asset," the employees. Admittedly, this brand of leadership can produce impressive results, but the shelf life of unwelcome styles is brief. Many organizations manage to dupe the general public when they report record-breaking profits and massive shareholder returns while masking dark and deceptive business practices and poor working conditions. Almost invariably, the truth works its way into the light.

The self-professed, "impulsive" founder and former CEO of Tesla, Elon Musk, is widely heralded as one of America's most successful leaders. The multi-billionaire innovator ascended to elite status among the world's top business leaders. But the fiery electric car manufacturer has recently come under scrutiny for poor factory conditions and abusive treatment of workers (Wong, 2017). Another division of the Musk empire, SolarCity, was sued by employees who blew the whistle about fake sales records that were created to boost the company's value (McCoy, 2018). The 2018 lawsuit seeks financial damages for wrongful termination, mishandling of sexual harassment claims, and age discrimination.

A 2018 Bloomberg Businessweek article detailed the cruel and unusual treatment of employees at a Tesla production facility, reportedly providing free Red Bull in order to keep employees awake to meet soaring production demands, and forcing employees to walk through raw sewage that spilled on the factory floor in order to keep production on schedule (Robinson and Faux, 2019). In fact, Elon Musk is known to have slept on the hard floors of the factory reportedly to signal to his employees his willingness to "feel their pain." In Musk's words, "whatever pain my employees were feeling, I wanted mine to be worse" (quoted in Wong, 2017). A noble gesture? Highly unlikely.

Given the eye-popping reports of unfair treatment of employees, disregard for sexual harassment claims, and the like, it's difficult to interpret Musk's words as anything but hypocrisy. Sleeping on the production floor as an attempt to relate to his employees also served as a perch (albeit an uncomfortable one) to watch over his employees. Given the volume of allegations levied against Tesla, and the widely reported indiscretions of its founder, it's hard to give them the benefit of the doubt.

The questionable business practices and alleged poor treatment of employees at Tesla are ghastly, and they expose the dark underbelly of organizational life. Oddly enough, given the horrid allegations that have been widely reported, one would expect to see a gaping misalignment between the core values and the reportedly unsavory business practices at Tesla. But you don't find words like trust, honesty, ethics, respect, and fairness among Tesla's core values. There is absolutely no word, phrase, or statement that suggests how Tesla's leadership intends to conduct business, or to demonstrate its commitment to the people that produce their transformative automobiles. Instead, the core values focus squarely on making a quality car:

1. **A Clean Start**

   As Tesla was founded in Silicon Valley, they will use a Silicon Valley approach which means moving fast and being innovative and creative.

2. **Committed to Electric**

   Tesla follows its mission to pursue sustainable energy, and offers EV's to fulfil a sustainable energy future.

3. **Build Around the Driver**

    Connect the car, driver, and environment.

4. **Sparking the Evolution**

    Develop unprecedented products, accelerating the world's transition to electric mobility, with providing affordable electric mobility (Model 3).

Prioritizing product values over cultural values is a recipe for disaster, and it is no surprise that Tesla has fallen fowl of public disapproval on more than one occasion.

THE ROAD TO HELL...

As people, we judge ourselves by our intentions. We judge others by their actions. We dismiss our own actions often by convincing ourselves that our intentions were just, fair, or honorable. And we condemn others while judging their actions as unjust, unfair, or dishonorable. We've all heard the popular phrase, "the road to hell is paved with good intentions." Leaders may have the best intentions as they pursue the company goals, but they often lose sight of the needs, values, and aspirations of their employees. When a leader fails to align their actions and behaviors to the core values of the company, the effects ripple throughout the organization. Employees are in constant watch mode, peering for any signs of the leader's true intentions. Leaders are rightfully judged by their actions. Intentions are obscure and irrelevant because the impact is the same.

Once a leader has lost the trust of employees, there's rarely a happy ending. Grievances, lawsuits, conflict, and attrition increase, while the morale, engagement, and performance of employees decrease. Since labor spending typically accounts for two-thirds of the profit and loss statement, it seems logical that leaders would naturally be inclined to do the hard work necessary to retain their most valuable "asset," employees. The cost of replacing an employee is estimated at 1.5x their salary. So, when we do the math, the return-on-investment for investing in employees by taking personal responsibility for aligning our actions and behaviors to the core values of the organization is immeasurable. The time for leaders to judge themselves by their actions is long overdue.

PEOPLE OVER PROFITS

It's time for the leadership discourse to emphasize people over profits. The relentless pursuit of maximum profits and a healthy return on investment has hijacked the moral conscience of leaders in pandemic proportions as they trade their values for profits and personal gain. If the general consensus among leaders is that profit trumps everything, employee morale be damned, then all references to valuing employees in the culture manifestos should be removed.

In this climate of the #MeToo Movement, Black Lives Matter, and the woke culture, truth-telling among leaders is no longer just a good idea, it's a business imperative. The millennial generation has ushered in a new and welcomed era of awareness and accountability, and the risk of exposure for illicit acts in this fast-moving social media world is tremendous. Leaders who fail to align their actions and behaviors to their personal and company values should be prepared for the inevitable reckoning that awaits.

A FINAL THOUGHT

Every organization has an ethos, a philosophy that is shaped by the values and principles of its founders. From mom-and-pop shops to corporate giants, it is essential that this philosophy is embraced and demonstrated by every member of the organization. The degree to which employees exhibit the company values largely depends on the actions and behaviors of the leaders. When leaders are willing to do the hard work necessary to lead ethically, transparently, and responsibly, an engaged, collaborative, results-oriented workforce is likely to emerge. But corporate values can be hijacked and misused by unscrupulous, selfish leaders when they prioritize their own self-interest over the needs and aspirations of employees. They exchange their moral conscience for profit and personal gain, at the employee's expense.

Conventional wisdom says that profit is the "bottom-line." This manner of thinking suggests that the ultimate goal of a leader is to achieve profit, at any cost. It is time for leaders to challenge this paradigm. People over profits is the new mantra. The business world has evolved toward a greater emphasis on the human component, and millennials, a group that now form the majority of the U.S. workforce, demand transparency, accountability, and ethical leadership. When leaders gain the trust of employees, the benefits to the organization are immeasurable.

ABOUT THE AUTHOR

Kendall is Sr. Vice President of Operations for a large contact center based in Ventura County, CA, and has garnered 30 years of experience in key leadership roles for companies such as AT&T, and Nationwide Insurance. He specializes in building and revitalizing world-class contact centers, and subscribes to a "people first" mentality. He firmly believes that a people-led approach is the key to corporate success, since profits and stability are natural outcomes of a dynamic, engaged workforce whose values are aligned with organizational goals.

Kendall holds several postgraduate qualifications, including a PhD in Industrial/Organizational Psychology from Northcentral University, an MA in Organization Management from the University of Phoenix, a BA in Organizational Behavior from National-Louis University, and a Certificate of Executive Leadership from Cornell University. He has taught management and leadership courses for Penn State University, University of Phoenix, and Fremont College.

Kendall is passionate about developing authentic leadership strategies and dispelling hypocrisy from corporate cultures, which is what inspired him to write "Visions, Values, and Corporate Hypocrisy." With his combined academic and corporate expertise, Kendall has a wealth of knowledge to share with aspiring leaders, and indeed with anyone interested in the subject of leadership. He currently lives in California, and is father to three young adults, Ryan, Reid, and Kayla Williams.

REFERENCES

Chapter 1

1. Gerson, M. (2016). The virtue of hypocrisy. *The Associated Press*. Retrieved August 22, 2020, from https://www.pilotonline.com/opinion/columns/article_9f31566f-aab4-5efa-aac5-cfec28d340f6.html

2. Sonnenberg, F. (2019). *23 ways to spot a hypocrite*. Retrieved November 12, 2020, from https://www.franksonnenbergonline.com/blog/23-ways-to-spot-a-hypocrite/

3. Bible Gateway. Retrieved August 22, 2020, from https://classic.biblegateway.com/passage/?search=Matthew+7&version=NIV

4. Hamilton, J. (2016). Wells Fargo is fined $185 million over unapproved accounts. *Bloomberg*. Retrieved November 12, 2020, from https://www.bloomberg.com/news/articles/2016-09-08/wells-fargo-fined-185-million-over-unwanted-customer-accounts

5. Wells Fargo Website. Retrieved October 10, 2020, from https://www.wellsfargo.com/about/corporate/

6. Bardella, K. (2020). Trump's Ebola obsession reveals the hypocrisy of his Coronavirus response now. *Euronews*. Retrieved November 12, 2020, from https://www.euronews.com/2020/03/11/trump-tweets-about-obama-coronavirus-ebola-reveal-hypocrisy-his-crisis-view

7. The Trump Twitter Archive. Retrieved September 04, 2021, from http://trumptwitterarchive.com/

8. Humphrey, N. (2011). *Soul dust: The magic of consciousness.* New York: Princeton University Press.

9. Stanford University Encyclopedia of Philosophy. (2019). Definition of Implicit bias. Retrieved November 12, 2020, from https://plato.stanford.edu/entries/implicit-bias/#toc

Chapter 2

1. Your best employees are leaving; but is it personal, or practical? (2018). *Randstad US.* Retrieved September 5, 2020, from https://rlc.randstadusa.com/press-room/press-releases/your-best-employees-are-leaving-but-is-it-personal-or-practical

2. Craig, W. (2014). What is company culture, and how do you change it? *Forbes Magazine.* Retrieved October 17, 2020, from https://www.forbes.com/sites/williamcraig/2014/10/24/what-is-company-culture-and-how-do-you-change-it/#76ad1f49b308

3. Shamira, B., & Eilam, G. (2005). "What's your story?" A life-stories approach to authentic leadership development. *The Leadership Quarterly* 16, 395-417.

4. Avolio, B.J., & Gardner, W.L. (2005). Authentic leadership development: Getting to the root of positive forms of leadership. *The Leadership Quarterly* 16, 315-338.

5. Epstein, K. (2019). Greta Thunberg wants you to listen to the scientists, not her. *The Washington Post*. Retrieved November 05, 2020, from https://www.sciencealert.com/greta-thunberg-wants-you-to-listen-to-scientists-not-her

6. Greta Thunberg's World Economic Forum 2019 Special Address. (2019). *Open Transcript*. Retrieved November 05, 2020, from http://opentranscripts.org/transcript/greta-thunberg-world-economic-forum-2019/

7. Schwantes, M. (2018). Delta CEO's latest truth-telling will only make the NRA stark raving mad. *Inc. Magazine*. Retrieved September 7, 2020, from https://www.inc.com/marcel-schwantes/deltas-ceo-says-he-wasnt-trying-to-be-a-politician-when-he-cut-ties-with-nra-real-reason-is-a-brilliant-leadership-move.html

8. Ambrosini, B. (2019). Somebody's gotta tell the freakin' truth: Jerry Falwell's aides break their silence. *Politico*. Retrieved August 29, 2020, from https://www.politico.com/magazine/story/2019/09/09/jerry-falwell-liberty-university-loans-227914

9. Greenbaum, R.L., Bardes-Mawritz, M., & Piccolo, R.F. (2015). How hypocritical leaders affect employee turnover. *Journal of Management*. Retrieved September 5, 2020, from https://www.ioatwork.com/hypocritical-leaders-affect-employee-turnover/

10. Kamena, G., & Blackmon, R. (2012). Authentic leaders: A rare and endangered species. *Maxwell Air Force Base.* Retrieved September 6, 2020, from https://www.maxwell.af.mil/news/Commentaries/Display/article/421493/authentic-leaders-a-rare-and-endangered-species/

11. Baker, M.G., Wilson, N., & Anglemyer, A. (2020). Successful elimination of Covid-19 transmission in New Zealand. *The New England Journal of Medicine.* Retrieved November 04, 2020, from https://www.nejm.org/doi/full/10.1056/NEJMc2025203

Chapter 3

1. Mallet, M., Nelson, B., & Steiner, C. (2012). The most annoying, pretentious, and useless business jargon. *Forbes Magazine.* Retrieved November 12, 2020, from https://www.forbes.com/sites/groupthink/2012/01/26/the-most-annoying-pretentious-and-useless-business-jargon/?sh=6dbe27bc2eea

2. Dvorak, N., & Nelson, B. (2016). Few employees believe in their company's values. *Business Journal.* Retrieved November 12, 2020, from https://news.gallup.com/businessjournal/195491/few-employees-believe-company-values.aspx

3. Balzer, M. (2018). What millennials want… Be fair, be honest, be real. *Thrive Global.* Retrieved November 12, 2020. https://thriveglobal.com/stories/what-millennials-want-be-fair-be-honest-be-real/

4. Mintz, S. (2012). Good leaders model underlying core ethical values in decision making. *Ethics Sage*. Retrieved August 29, 2020, from, https://www.ethicssage.com/2012/04/good-lleaders-model-underlying-core-ethical-values-in-decision-making.html

5. Rio, J. (2017). The North Star: Polaris. *Space.com*. Retrieved November 12, 2020, from https://www.space.com/15567-north-star-polaris.html

6. Harter, J. (2019). Why some leaders have their employee's trust, and some don't. *Gallup Workplace*. Retrieved November 12, 2020, from https://www.gallup.com/workplace/258197/why-leaders-employees-trust-don.aspx

7. Hollon, J. (2016). The research is clear: Few employees believe in their company's values. *Checkster, Better Talent Decisions*. Retrieved August 29, 2020, from https://www.checkster.com/blog/2016/09/15/the-reseach-is-clear-few-employees-believe-in-their-companys-values

Chapter 4

1. Merriam-Webster. Definition of microaggression. Retrieved September 30, 2020, from https://www.merriam-webster.com/dictionary/microaggression

2. Cillizza, C. (2019). The remarkably casual sexism of Donald Trump. *CNN Politics*. Retrieved January 04,

2021, from https://edition.cnn.com/2019/10/02/politics/donald-trump-kirstjen-nielsen/index.html

3. Finley, L. and Esposito, L. (2019). The Immigrant as Bogeyman: Examining Donald Trump and the Right's Anti-immigrant, Anti-PC Rhetoric. *Humanity & Society*, 44(2). Retrieved January 04, 2021, from https://journals.sagepub.com/doi/full/10.1177/0160597619832627

4. Washington , E.F., Birch, A.H., & and Roberts, L.M. (2020). When and how to respond to microaggressions. *Harvard Business Review*. Retrieved September 30, 2020, from https://hbr.org/2020/07/when-and-how-to-respond-to-microaggressions

5. CNN Business. (2019). Anderson Cooper and Monika Bickert interview. Retrieved January 04, 2021, from https://edition.cnn.com/videos/tech/2019/05/25/facebook-monika-bickert-pelosi-video-cooper-intv-sot-ac360-vpx.cnn

6. Isaac, M. and Shane, S. (2017). Facebook's Russia-linked ads came in many disguises. *The New York Times*. Retrieved January 05, 2021, from https://www.nytimes.com/2017/10/02/technology/facebook-russia-ads-.html

7. Mayer, J. (2019). The Case of Al Franken: A close look at the accusations against the former senator. *The New*

Yorker. Retrieved January 04, 2021, from https://www.newyorker.com/magazine/2019/07/29/the-case-of-al-franken

8. Valenti, J. (2017). Mike Pence doesn't eat alone with women: That speaks volumes. *The Guardian*. Retrieved January 04, 2021, from https://www.theguardian.com/commentisfree/2017/mar/31/mike-pence-doesnt-eat-alone-women-speaks-volumes

Chapter 5

1. Merriam-Webster. Definition of woke. Retrieved November 07, 2020, from https://www.merriam-webster.com/dictionary/woke

2. *The Dove Self-Esteem Project*. Retrieved October 01, 2020, from https://www.dove.com/us/en/dove-self-esteem-project/our-mission.html

3. Young, S. (2019). Marks and Spencer launches LGBT+ sandwich to raise money for charity – but has it divided opinion. *The Independent*. Retrieved January 05, 2021, from https://www.independent.co.uk/life-style/marks-and-spencer-lgbt-sandwich-charity-reaction-twitter-a8897631.html

4. Taylor, C. (2019). Why Gillette's new ad campaign is toxic. *Forbes*. Retrieved January 05, 2021, from https://www.

forbes.com/sites/charlesrtaylor/2019/01/15/why-gillettes-new-ad-campaign-is-toxic/?sh=69e76fd25bc9

Chapter 6

1. McCullough, I. (2014). Did Mozilla CEO Brendan Eich deserve to be removed from his position? *Forbes*. Retrieved November 20, 2020, from https://www.forbes.com/sites/quora/2014/04/11/did-mozilla-ceo-brendan-eich-deserve-to-be-removed-from-his-position-due-to-his-support-for-proposition-8/?sh=69ca723e2158

2. Shankland, S. (2014). Mozilla under fire: Inside the 9-day reign of fallen CEO Brendan Eich. *Cnet*. Retrieved January 05, 2021, from https://www.cnet.com/news/mozilla-under-fire-inside-the-9-day-reign-of-fallen-ceo-brendan-eich/

3. Lawrence, A. (2019). The NFL is 70% black, so why is its TV coverage so white? *The Guardian*. Retrieved October 01, 2020, from https://www.theguardian.com/sport/2019/jan/31/nfl-tv-coverage-racial-demographics-super-bowl

4. Reed, S. (2019). NFL earns lowest score for racial, gender hiring in 15 years. *abc News*, October 30. Retrieved November 20, 2020, from https://abcnews.go.com/Sports/wireStory/nfl-earns-lowest-score-racial-gender-hiring-15-66640048

5. NFL mission and values statement. Retrieved January 05, 2021, from https://www.nfl.com/news/mission-and-values

6. Curtis, C. (2020). A reminder of what Colin Kaepernick actually said, and a timeline of his actions. *USA Today*. Retrieved January 05, 2021, from https://ftw.usatoday.com/2020/06/colin-kaepernick-anthem-protest-timeline-message

7. Martin, S. and Mchendry, G.F. (2016). Kaepernick's stand: Patriotism, protest, and professional sports. *ResearchGate*. Retrieved January 05, 2021, from https://www.researchgate.net/publication/335942115_Kaepernick%27s_Stand_Patriotism_Protest_and_Professional_Sports

8. Blow, C.M. (2017). The flag is drenched with our blood. *The New York Times*. Retrieved January 05, 2021, from https://www.nytimes.com/2017/09/28/opinion/the-flag-is-drenched-with-our-blood.html

Chapter 7

1. Affirmative action in the United States. *Wikipedia*. Retrieved October 01, 2020, from https://en.wikipedia.org/wiki/Affirmative_action_in_the_United_States#cite_note-14e

2. Goetz, L. (2020). Sheryl Sandberg's success story. *Investopedia*. Retrieved November 20, 2020, from https://www.investopedia.com/articles/insights/051416/sheryl-

sandbergs-success-story-net-worth-education-top-quotes.asp

3. Ellis-Peterson, H. (2019). Burger King removes 'racist' ad showing man trying to eat with giant chopsticks. *The Guardian*. Retrieved January 05, 2021, from https://www.theguardian.com/business/2019/apr/09/burger-king-removes-racist-ad-showing-man-trying-to-eat-with-giant-chopsticks

4. Bulman, M. (2018). H&M apologises following backlash over 'racist' image of child model on website. *The Independent*. Retrieved January 05, 2021, from https://www.independent.co.uk/news/uk/home-news/hm-apology-racist-image-website-child-model-backlash-twitter-monkey-jumper-black-a8147641.html

Chapter 8

1. Adam Barone, A. (2020). What is an asset? *Investopedia*. Retrieved November 20, 2020, from https://www.investopedia.com/terms/a/asset.asp

2. Adkins, A. (2016). Employee engagement in the U.S. stagnant in 2015. *Gallup*. Retrieved November 20, 2020, from https://news.gallup.com/poll/188144/employee-engagement-stagnant-2015.aspx

3. Peakon website. (2019). *Peakon releases world's largest ever study on employee feedback, based on 11 million responses from 160 countries*. Retrieved November 20, 2020, from https://peakon.com/press/press-releases/peakon-releases-

worlds-largest-ever-study-on-employee-feedback-based-on-11-million-responses-from-160-countries/

4. U.S. Labour Statistics. (2020). *Time use of millennials and non-millennials*. Retrieved November 20, 2020, from https://www.bls.gov/opub/mlr/2019/article/time-use-of-millennials-and-nonmillennials.html

5. Pink, D. (2011). *Drive: The surprising truth about what motivates us*. New York: Riverhead Books.

6. Flowers, V.S., & Hughes, C.L. (1973). Why employees stay. *Harvard Business Review*. Retrieved November 05, 2020, from https://hbr.org/1973/07/why-employees-stay

Chapter 9

1. Ibbetson, R. (2020). Jeff Bezos' $10bn pledge to fight climate change is slammed as a 'greenwash' by critics who say Amazon pumps out massive amounts of carbon AND avoids hundreds of millions in tax. *Mail Online*. Retrieved November 20, 2020, from https://www.dailymail.co.uk/news/article-8015509/Jeff-Bezos-10bn-pledge-fight-climate-change-slammed-greenwash-critics.html

2. Amazon' leadership principles. Retrieved January 05, 2021, from https://www.aboutamazon.com/about-us/leadership-principles

Chapter 10

1. Grant, A. (2014). The dark side of emotional intelligence. *The Atlantic*. Retrieved November 20, 2020, from https://www.theatlantic.com/health/archive/2014/01/the-dark-side-of-emotional-intelligence/282720/

2. Menges, J., Kilduff, M., Kern, S., & Bruch, H. (2015). The awestruck effect: Followers suppress emotion expression in response to charismatic but not individually considerate leadership. *The Leadership Quarterly*. Retrieved November 20, 2020, from https://www.researchgate.net/publication/279737449_The_awestruck_effect_Followers_suppress_emotion_expression_in_response_to_charismatic_but_not_individually_considerate_leadership

Chapter 11

1. Hudson, Z. Leadership. (n.d.). *Passing the Baton Leadership Podcast*. Retrieved November 05, 2020, from https://www.passingthebatonpodcast.com/are-your-morals-for-sale/

2. Obeso, I., Moisa, M., Ruff, C.C., & Dreher, J. (2018). A causal role for right temporo-parietal junction in signalling moral conflict. Retrieved November 05, 2020, from https://elifesciences.org/articles/40671

3. Chow, D. (2013). Believe or deceiver? Why liars are difficult to sniff out. *Live Science*. Retrieved November 20, 2020, from https://www.livescience.com/37023-lying-deception-psychology.html

4. Mann, S., Vrij, A., & Bull, R. (2004). Detecting true lies: Police officers' ability to detect suspects' lies. *Journal of Applied Psychology*, 89(1), 137-49.

5. McVeigh, K. (2020). Coca-Cola, Pepsi and Nestlé named top plastic polluters for third year in a row. *The Guardian*. Retrieved January 05, 2021, from https://www.theguardian.com/environment/2020/dec/07/coca-cola-pepsi-and-nestle-named-top-plastic-polluters-for-third-year-in-a-row

6. Hankin, A. (2019). A dozen or so companies Amazon is slaying this year. *Investopedia*. Retrieved January 05, 2021, from https://www.investopedia.com/news/5-companies-amazon-killing/

7. Lee Yohn, D. (2020). Amazon faces a crucible moment with employees. *Forbes*. Retrieved January 05, 2021, from https://www.forbes.com/sites/deniselyohn/2020/06/02/amazon-faces-a-crucible-moment-with-employees/?sh=26a3b8a23822

8. Martin, D. (2017). Dow Chemical pushes White House to kill risk study showing pesticide dangers. *Nbcnews*. Retrieved January 05, 2021, from https://www.nbcnews.com/news/us-news/dow-chemical-pushes-white-house-kill-risk-study-showing-pesticide-n749396

9. Smith, A. (2016). Morgan Stanley to pay $3.2 billion for its role in market meltdown. *CNN Business*. Retrieved January 05, 2021, from https://money.cnn.com/2016/02/11/news/

companies/morgan-stanley-mortgage-backed-securities/index.html

10. Obeso, I., Moisa, M., Ruff, C.C., & Dreher, J. (2018). A causal role for right temporo-parietal junction in signalling moral conflict. *U.S. Institute of National Health*. Retrieved November 20, 2020, from https://www.ncbi.nlm.nih.gov/pmc/articles/PMC6298767/

11. Thomas, Z. (2016). What's in Donald Trump's tax returns? *BBC News*. Retrieved January 05, 2021, from https://www.bbc.co.uk/news/election-us-2016-36382410

Chapter 12

1. McCoy, K. (2018). Lawsuit: SolarCity employees created fake sales records that boosted the company's value. *USA Today*. Retrieved November 20, 2020, from https://www.usatoday.com/story/money/2018/10/12/lawsuit-says-solarcity-employees-created-fake-sales-records-boosting-value/863647002/

2. Robinson, M., & Faux, Z. (2019). When Elon Musk tried to destroy a Tesla whistleblower. *Bloomberg Business Week*. Retrieved November 20, 2020, from https://www.bloomberg.com/news/features/2019-03-13/when-elon-musk-tried-to-destroy-tesla-whistleblower-martin-tripp

www.ingramcontent.com/pod-product-compliance
Lightning Source LLC
LaVergne TN
LVHW011840060526
838200LV00054B/4118